EXTREME CARS

Stephen Vokins

EXTREME CARS

Dedication

This book is dedicated to my parents, and to all the teachers who pressed on in their efforts to educate me, even when it may have appeared at the time that those efforts were not always adequately rewarded.

First published in September 2005

A catalogue record for this book is available from the British Library

ISBN 1 84425 225 6

Whilst the publisher has made every effort to trace copyright ownership of photographs, this has not proved possible in every case. If a copyright owner has inadvertently been offended, then please do discuss the matter with the Editorial Director of the Books Division at Haynes Publishing.

Library of Congress catalog card no. 2005926086

Published by Haynes Publishing, Sparkford, Yeovil, Somerset BA22 7JJ, UK

Tel: 01963 442030 Fax: 01963 440001
Int. tel: +44 1963 442030 Int. fax: +44 1963 440001
E-mail: sales@haynes.co.uk
Website: www.haynes.co.uk

Haynes North America Inc.
861 Lawrence Drive, Newbury Park,
California 91320, USA

Designed by G&M Designs Limited,
Raunds, Northamptonshire
Printed and bound in Great Britain by
J.H. Haynes & Co. Ltd, Sparkford

CONTENTS

FOREWORD

by Nick Mason, car collector, Pink Floyd drummer

I have always had a fascination for the history of the motor car, and it is made all the more captivating by the existence of vehicles which for one reason or another are worthy of the title 'Extreme'.

Cars can be extreme in a number of different ways, the most obvious of which is the capability of some to travel with indecent haste. To describe cars such as the Tiger T100 with its two Kawasaki ZX900 motorcycle engines as anything other than extreme would undoubtedly be an understatement, whilst the AMC Pacer and the Chinese Saint Horse Angel can equally be described as extreme cars, albeit for very different reasons.

It is no secret that my own particular motoring passion is for very fast cars, and I was therefore delighted to see some of my own favourite kings of speed appear in this excellent book. The McLaren F1, Ferrari Enzo, and Porsche 959 should be undisputed entries, whilst cars such as the Ultima CanAm and the Rinspeed Roaster SC-R may not be as well known but are equally deserving of a mention.

Other treasures to be found in this book are the peerless Ferrari 250 GTO, the Bugatti Royale, and the Cadillac V16, all of which are obvious entries when talking about the extremes of perfection. But these are not the only extremes explored within these pages: extremes of size, fuel consumption, and frightfulness make the book an entertaining, and at times, surprising read.

This is, I believe, a book that will appeal equally to the lovers of fast cars and the casually interested. It features a number of true classics – a word often used unwisely to describe any car over 15 years old, but here it applies to genuine machinery of timeless quality – as well as some truly daft cars and a few real horrors.

Perhaps the greatest surprise, however, is the final car featured (page 142) – a car I had never previously considered as outstanding in any particular area. I am sure you, too, will find cars to amuse and entertain in this celebration of the furthest extremities of car design.

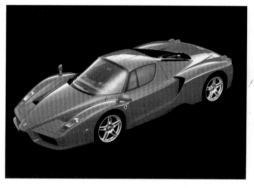

INTRODUCTION

Cars are about transport. Their role is to get people from A to B in comfort, safely and reliably. We all know that. And in an ideal world – or perhaps, more accurately, a car-hater's utopia – that is the only function of a car, and on that judgement every example should stand or fall. In the real world, however, where ego, marketing, and human nature seek to pervert such absolutes, cars fulfil many more roles than that of mere transportation.

A car is a piece of street sculpture, and in some cases could even be termed a work of art. It is also a haven into which one can retreat from the harshness of life whilst moving from one point to another. It is a statement of its owner's wealth and status (or lack of) within society. It can be an object of desire, or, in the case of a few particularly unfortunate examples, of ridicule. Speed, and the ability to shrink mileage, is something by which many in the real world judge a car's true potential. Its ability to transport its passengers safely and with a degree of dependability is, naturally, also an important consideration when judging a car. The levels of luxury afforded is yet another variable.

It should come as no surprise, therefore, that while many cars are distinctly humdrum and mediocre, blending into a dull and nondescript cityscape with consummate ease, there will always be some which stand out from the crowd and demand a double-take from even the most disinterested of passers-by. Such cars, varying – often wildly – from the norm, can be looked upon as extreme cars, and 250 examples of such abnormality are featured within the pages of this book. They are all instantly memorable, for a wide variety of differing but ultimately indisputable reasons. They reflect the personalities not only of those keen enough to court controversy by designing, making, or buying them, but also, more importantly, they represent the deep-seated desire within the human psyche to make a statement, by being different and individual.

Ownership of such a machine guarantees attention from onlookers. In a world where conformity is the safe option, the builders and subsequent owners of such vehicles should be saluted as brave, heroic, and supporters of the concept of street art. Whilst not all of the examples covered in this book could be classed as aesthetically pleasing or artistic, their fundamental difference from the norm is worthy of note. In such circumstances belonging to the extremes is praiseworthy, and it is this that is celebrated within the following pages.

CHAPTER ONE

"WHAT'LL SHE DO,

ARIEL ATOM 2

▼ 'This is the Atom. What you see is what you get – if it doesn't need it, it hasn't got it.' Possibly not the most obvious way of selling a car, but the Ariel Atom is such a focused, no frills piece of extreme motoring that this slogan sums up the real essence of the car most succinctly.

A stripped-to-the-bones two-seater road-going racer which has minimal bodywork and a correspondingly minuscule weight of just 450kg, it was described by motoring hack Jeremy Clarkson as 'motoring Nirvana'. Fitted with a 2-litre Honda VTEC engine, it beat all the established champions of super-fast road cars – such as the Porsche Boxster, Lamborghini Murcielago, Noble M12, and even the Porsche 911 GT3 – in a contest to establish the fastest lap of Rockingham Raceway, with a time of just 1 minute 17.6 seconds.

Launched in July 2003, the British designed and built Ariel Atom is a small car from an even smaller company, based in Somerset, which has all the big boys beaten at their own game.

ASTON MARTIN VANQUISH S

▶ Aston Martin is a permanent member of the supercar club comprised of names such as Ferrari, Lamborghini, and Porsche. Its cars are always breathtakingly fast, nearly always supremely elegant (a rare exception being the mid-1980s Zagato-bodied Virage), and understated, epitomising Britishness. They have certain defining design details, such as the shape of the radiator grille, which are a visual acceptance of the enviable heritage of the marque, and yet each new model takes forward the concept of Gran Tourismo motoring without being caught and held hostage to the past.

The 2004 Vanquish S is a fine example of this, being devastatingly suave, sophisticated, and yet brutally fast at the same time. Costing £174,000, its 5.9-litre V12 engine develops 520bhp, demolishing the first 62mph in 4.8 seconds and carrying its discerning occupants in fine luxury all the way up to a top speed of 200mph.

LANCIA THEMA 832

▶ One of the benefits of being a company within a larger conglomerate is that from time to time a degree of robbing from the corporate parts-bin can produce something very special, without incurring great cost.

Lancia found to their delight that belonging to Fiat gave them access to some very tasty oily bits indeed, and they were able to give a welcome image boost to the Thema, turning it into a wild, tyre-shredding beast by slotting under the bonnet a 3-litre, 215bhp Ferrari V8 engine, as used in the Ferrari 308, and wait for the orders to pour in. Cracking the 0–60 sprint in 7.2 seconds was highly pleasing, as was the top speed of 132mph, but the on-the-road price of almost £38,000 before options ensured that this was a purchase made on the advice of the heart and not the head, especially considering the highly upsetting rate of depreciation owners could expect to suffer.

Built for just two years between 1988–90, the Lancia Thema 832 was a fabulous car to drive, or to persuade your employer to give you as a company car, but as an ownership proposition, it was akin to contracting the plague.

MISTER?"

BENTLEY HUNAUDIERES

▲ 1999 was a good year for lovers of ultimate dream cars, for no other reason than that it was the year the Bentley Hunaudieres broke cover for the first time. It was named after the straight at Le Mans, where Bentley won five times between 1924 and 1930 and established the company's racing pedigree.

This was no ordinary concept, and no ordinary Bentley, if such a car can be said to exist. The Hunaudieres was a mid-engined two-seater supercar whose underpinnings could be traced back to the Lamborghini Diablo. It came complete with the mother of all engines sitting longitudinally behind the cockpit: an 8-litre, 64-valve W16 capable of delivering a more than adequate 623bhp through its four-wheel drive system, and capable of hurling the British Racing Green missile on to a top speed of 218mph.

Built using large amounts of carbon-fibre, the car was in most areas most un-Bentley like, and although the seats were trimmed in Connolly hide the dash was faced in turned aluminium, like a late 1920s racer, rather than walnut.

NISSAN SKYLINE GTR

▶ 1998's Nissan Skyline GTR is a car held in the greatest of awe by boy-racers the world over. It has been developed and modified many times over, and is seen by many as the king of the traffic-light grand prix: a poor man's Ferrari.

As one might expect from Japan, even in standard form the car bristles with technology, including four-wheel steering to eliminate excessive understeer when being driven in a hooligan manner. For similar occasions, speed sensors, lateral g-force sensors, throttle opening sensors, and brake light monitoring inputs are all fed into a computer which updates 100 times per second the amount of work required by the stability control systems to keep the car from making an undignified exit from the road via a hedge or shop window.

PORSCHE 959

▶ The late 1980s was a period of excess, where bigger, faster, and more expensive were all seen as indicators of superiority, and Porsche, who had hitherto built cars that were greatly desired but generally understated, felt the need to be on the bandwagon.

When Porsche set out to do something they usually do it better than most, so it came as little surprise when they launched the 959 to learn that it could reach almost 200mph, had four-wheel-drive, and was powered by a slightly de-tuned and more road-friendly version of the racing engine from the 962. Its styling was unusually extravagant for Porsche, and appeared to have been influenced by the hugely over-the-top Ferrari Testarossa, which was not to everyone's taste; but as only 200 examples of the 959 were built, including the examples that won the 1989 Paris Dakar rally, there were always going to be more would-be punters than cars, thus guaranteeing its status as an instant classic.

PAGANI ZONDA C12

◀ Whilst many of the world's fastest cars are among the most beautiful, good looks are not essential, and sheer brute force and power can often win a vehicle the title 'supercar' whilst its appearance can be highly controversial. One such car was the Bugatti EB110, and another is the undeniably powerful Pagani Zonda C12 of 1999.

Powered by a Mercedes-Benz AMG 7.3-litre V12 which develops 555bhp, pushing the £360,000 mid-engined super machine from standstill to 60mph in 3.9 seconds, it can go on to a top speed of 210mph. If power and ultimate performance are at the top of the shopping list, then the Zonda deserves a place on it, although it shares the list with some cars of considerably better appearance.

RENAULT ALPINE GTA V6

◄ The Renault Alpine GTA was a staggeringly handsome, hand-built machine with a fabricated steel chassis onto which was fitted a purposeful, mean-looking, and ultra-slippery (0.28cd) low-drag body made from glass-fibre. It used a rear-mounted 2,485cc turbo-charged V6 engine, which delivered 200bhp and was a tuned version of the engine from the more family-orientated Renault 25. It was capable of a top speed of 155mph, reaching the first 60mph in just 7 seconds.

Launched at the Amsterdam Motor Show in 1984, it took a further two years to cross the Channel, going on sale in the UK in right-hand-drive form in 1986, where it received much well-earned praise for its looks and performance.

RINSPEED ROADSTER SC-R

▼ The Roaster SC-R was a mean-looking sports car that was first shown to the public at the 1995 Geneva Motor Show, home turf for the famous Swiss design house of its creator, Rinspeed.

With an aluminium body fitted to a steel chassis, it was light, and with the supercharged 5-litre V8 Ford engine lurking under its low bonnet and pushing out a highly respectable 305bhp to its rear wheels, it was quick also. It could reach 60mph in a hair-raising 4.4 seconds, and its top speed was a full 160mph.

Its muscular bodywork was neatly adorned with tasteful chrome additions, such as the 18in wheels, side exhaust, grille, and roll-over hoops, whilst the cockpit was trimmed in exclusive leather, and bespoke luggage was available from De Shama.

STEALTH B6

▶ It must have been late one evening when the designers of the Stealth (launched in 2002) got around to naming their road-going, street-legal racer, as it would appear that on that occasion their sense of irony was working overtime: stealth is not a quality one could readily attribute to this car.

Powered by a 6.3-litre V8 Chevrolet engine, heavily tweaked to push out 511bhp, its blistering performance is accompanied by a howling symphony of mechanical screams as it rips its way towards the horizon and its top speed of just short of 240mph.

Its carbon-fibre bodywork is obviously designed for racing, and with its low centre of gravity, low weight, and mid-engined layout it performs very well on the track. Unlike most cars in its racing category, however, it is also able to return home without needing to ride on a trailer.

ULTIMA CANAM

▼ Traditionally, many kit cars have been inferior machines of variable quality, often copying classic designs and selling in penny numbers to enthusiasts who want the real thing but don't have the budget.

The Ultima CanAm, whilst undeniably a kit car, is none of the above, but is a serious vehicle with very serious performance. Built around a steel chassis, its glass-fibre bodywork is reminiscent of Le Mans race-cars, and its performance is similar. Powered by a 6.3-litre V8 Chevrolet engine which the builder can tune to give out over 600bhp, it is capable of the 0–60 sprint in 3.3 seconds, and a top speed of around 180mph. Buying the kit (which, apart from the various components, includes a 200-page manual and photo CD) costs around £35,000, and the build for an averagely competent home-mechanic can take up to a year.

FORD ESCORT COSWORTH

◄ 1992 was a vintage year for lovers of fast Fords, as this was the year that saw the arrival of one of the all-time great Ford cars in full road-going spec. Although badged an Escort, the basis of the Cosworth was actually a cut-down Sierra Cosworth 4x4 platform, with Escort-like panels stretched to fit. And whilst on the subject of bodywork, one of its more noticeable features had to be the huge double-whale-tail spoiler on the boot, which, in unspoken terms, said to any driver behind, 'Don't bother, you'll only look foolish if you try to pass.'

In standard ex-factory trim, the 2-litre four-cylinder engine put out 210bhp to the four-wheel-drive system, and gave a top speed of 140mph; but this was a de-tuned rally car, and many owners took it upon themselves to find the full 400bhp available to the competition examples with extra mods.

Sky-high insurance premiums – due not only to the performance offered but mainly to it becoming the car of choice for stealing and joyriding – ensured that only limited numbers ever sold, and today they are highly sought after.

MERCEDES-BENZ CLK GTR

▼ The problem with building supercars is that no sooner have you built the unquestioned *über* supercar than someone comes along and out-*übers* you. What was super-fast last week is this week merely fast. The bar keeps rising, which can be very depressing to a manufacturer spending many millions developing a car for a strictly limited number of very fickle customers keen to buy the latest superlative.

So when Mercedes-Benz, the descendants of the inventor of the car, decided to enter this high-cost, ultra-exclusive arena, they set out to establish a benchmark so far in advance of everything that had preceded it that their offering would go unchallenged for as long as possible. Enter the CLK GTR, a £1 million ultimate car. Derived from their highly successful GT1 class racer, the AMG-tuned 6.9-litre 191mph V12 600bhp road-legal racer was launched in 1998. In total, just 25 road cars were built.

PORSCHE CARRERA GT

▲ Long before boys grow up to become interested in girls, beer, and work, one word that looms large in their lexicon is Porsche. The German company has for many decades made the sports and racing cars about which all boys dream and which some go on to own.

The most extreme Porsche to date is, without doubt, the 2004 Carrera GT, a car which can reduce grown men to the drooling schoolboys they once were, and hardened motoring journalists to grovelling sycophants. Its 5.7-litre V10 engine delivers a supercar 605bhp, and with its racing pedigree no one dare question the supremacy of this, the latest new kid on the block. With a top speed of 208mph (the first 60mph coming up in 3.9 seconds) it can certainly hold its head high, whilst the $440,000 price tag ensures that it will never become the boy-racers' tool of choice. Loaded with the very latest in high-tech, including composite body-panels, ceramic brake discs and clutch-plates, a total of just 1,500 will be built.

PLYMOUTH ROAD RUNNER SUPERBIRD

▼ 1970 was a good year to be young, American, and affluent. It was the only year during which one could walk into a Plymouth dealer and drive out in the race-developed road-legal Superbird. Based on a base two-door Road Runner, its rudimentary aerodynamic package included a wedge-shaped nose added to the front and probably the highest rear spoiler ever fitted to a car. A 7.2-litre V8 developing 390bhp mated to a four-speed manual gearbox did the honours under the bonnet. For a little extra cash you could even ask the nice man to fit disc brakes to the front, replacing the standard-fit drums and increasing your chances of surviving the ownership experience.

Not only did the car look startling, its performance was not far short of ludicrously dangerous. The racing cars were capable of 220mph, whilst the street machines could easily see the wrong side of 150mph. So successful was the Superbird on the racetracks of America that the regulations were hurriedly redrawn to exclude it from further competition, and once it was no longer of use to Plymouth for PR-boosting races it was withdrawn from production.

"WHAT'LL SHE DO, MISTER?"

FORD INDIGO

▶ On first acquaintance one could be forgiven for thinking the IndiGo was a concept from the drawing boards at Maranello. But this was no Ferrari, even though its performance was what might be expected from one.

Launched in 1996, Ford were happy for people to note the Formula 1 inspirations, such as its carbon-fibre bodywork, large spoilers, and ability to impress with exciting speeds. A top speed of 170mph was possible, with the first 60mph reached in less than 4 seconds, powered by its 441bhp mid-mounted 6-litre V12. Whilst obviously too radical for road use in its original form, Ford were keen to point out that producing a high performance road car based on the IndiGo was feasible. As yet, they have chosen not to prove this point, much to the chagrin of the car's many admirers.

AC SUPERBLOWER

▼ No book written on the subject of supercars could get by without mentioning the AC Cobra, the car that for many years was listed by the *Guinness Book of Records* as the fastest production car in the world. It first gained notoriety in 1964 when one was driven on Britain's M1 motorway at 185mph, testing prior to a trip to Le Mans. The outcry resulting from this eventually resulted in the country's none-too-exciting 70mph limit being imposed.

The Superblower is the latest version of this iconic legend that had originally started out as the AC Ace, and is certainly a worthy descendant. Its 5-litre supercharged V8 engine develops 320bhp, which gives the open-topped wild thing a top speed of 165mph. Admittedly there are faster cars out there, with more sophisticated chassis and, crucially, better aerodynamics, but this is the car that was featured as a poster on the bedroom walls of all the modern designers whose cars are now faster, while they were still growing up. The AC will always be held in the highest esteem by lovers of fast cars, for its legendary status, its swooping, beautiful, hand-built bodywork, and the sheer menacing growl of its uncomplicated and yet ultra-powerful 427cu in engine.

MERCEDES-BENZ SLR McLAREN

▶ SLR are three initials that, when put together, have a very special meaning. They evoke memories of the Silver Arrows road-racer from the 1950s, the 300 SLR driven by Stirling Moss in the 1955 Mille Miglia. So when, in 2004, the Stuttgart company decided to deploy them once more on a car, it had to be a very special sort of car. And the SLR McLaren is just that.

The awesome styling that initially attracts one's eye mixes F1 with boulevard cruiser: here is a car driven by a 5.4-litre supercharged V8 engine that delivers a mouth-watering 625bhp and a top speed of 210mph, but is nevertheless a nice car to be in. This is a supercar for people who can afford one but have taken slightly longer to amass the necessary funds than intended, and now find themselves less agile than they were. Entry into the cabin via the semi gullwing doors is not too demanding, and once inside there is plush leather, aluminium, and comfort. This car sets out to show that supercar performance does not mean life has to be uncomfortable. It also shows, however, that not all super-smooth looking cars are mere pussycats.

McLAREN F1

▶ The McLaren F1 is the name any schoolboy expert will utter in reverent tones if asked to say which is the best, fastest, or coolest car ever made. Perhaps the reason this car won so many hearts, and not just those too young to drive, was that it was designed by the best brains in the business, using crisp, clean sheets of paper, with people standing directly behind them with open cheque books and a willingness to keep doling out the necessary funds until it was finished.

The figures surrounding this almost mythological car seem to be the stuff of fiction, and yet they are all fact: a top speed of 240.1mph, 0–60 in 3.2 seconds, 6-litre V12 BMW engine delivering 627bhp, purchase price in excess of £650,000 …

Starting with a clean sheet of paper resulted in the driver sitting in the middle, a monocoque body built of carbon-fibre, and an engine bay lined with 24-carat gold leaf. However, of the planned build of 350 less than 100 were ever produced (between 1993 and 1997), as the financial crash at the end of the 1980s had robbed McLaren of the kind of customer willing and able to invest that sort of money in a car.

DODGE VIPER SRT/10

▼ In production since 1996, the Dodge Viper is a true American muscle car, whose 8.2-litre V10 engine (which started out in life powering trucks) delivers a full 500bhp and a top speed of 190mph, reaching 60mph from standstill in less than 4 seconds. Such extreme performance is remarkable in any car, but in the Viper it is further enhanced by a truly threatening appearance that lives up to its namesake reptile.

Costing $82,295, this is no impulse purchase, but those who choose the Viper will never be short of fun. Its front wheels are 18in in diameter and the rears 19, and around town, where enviable glances should abound, the owner can expect to average a disappointing 12mpg. On the open road, however, if the chance presents itself, the experience resulting from a firm prod on the throttle pedal with a heavy right foot is truly electrifying.

LAMBORGHINI COUNTACH

▲ The Lamborghini Countach was the dream car of every schoolboy throughout the 1970s and well into the 1980s. Its dramatic and extreme shape, so skilfully penned by Marcello Gandini, was revolutionary and exciting, and, uniquely, actually got better as it grew older and spoilers were added and the most outrageous and extreme rear spoiler ever to grace a car. Its extremely low, two-seater cockpit was accessed via scissor doors, and once inside the only view that was any good was directly in front.

With the 5-litre, 455bhp V12 fired up, the huge, unwieldy beast was hard to drive and could be very intimidating, with seriously heavy controls and poor visibility, but as speeds rose everything became easier. This, despite its monumentally extrovert presence, was definitely no car for poseurs, and only truly rewarded those brave enough to open up its vast reserves of performance. 0–60mph in 4.9 seconds was very fast for its time and is still highly respectable today, while its top speed of approximately 180mph (every car tested appeared to give slightly different results) was captivating.

HONDA NSX

◄ Over the course of the first three-quarters of the 20th century, an elite clique of European manufacturers established for themselves the supercar market. With their wealth of experience, much of it gained on the world's racetracks, they felt pretty invulnerable to attack from other manufacturers. That is, until Honda – using their experience gained on F1 circuits, and benefiting from the knowledge of Ayrton Senna – launched the NSX in 1991.

The NSX was a supercar for people who had the money but were intimidated by the levels of skill needed to drive one. Powered by a mid-car mounted 3-litre V6 and capable of 160mph, it was docile in normal driving conditions and was as easy to drive in the rush hour as it was to drive at break-neck speeds around the Nürburgring. This was a serious attempt by Honda to break into the lucrative supercar sector, but ultimately the badge cachet of the likes of Ferrari, Lamborghini, Porsche *et al*, kept many European customers away from the doors of the Honda dealerships, and the NSX never achieved the sales success its creators had hoped for.

BUGATTI TYPE 35

◄ The Type 35 Bugatti was a legendary racer with a stunning competition record that made its debut appearance at the 1924 French Grand Prix. Supremely elegant and light, it was the exact opposite of the approach W.O. Bentley took to building his racing cars, and as a result Ettore Bugatti was famously quoted as saying 'Senor Bentley builds the fastest trucks in the world.'

With some examples even fitted with superchargers, the lightweight two-seater was a great success. It was an extremely pretty car, complete with its cast aluminium wheels (made by a process kept secret to this day) and trademark horseshoe radiator. The attention to detail went beyond what was strictly necessary, as the engine bay was a beautiful piece of craftsmanship, with the cylinder head and block all beautifully turned, looking more like the workings of an expensive watch than a sports car engine.

Today, Type 35s are highly prized among collectors, and examples with racing history are particularly valued.

TIGER T100

◄ Ever since Karl Benz and Gottlieb Daimler invented the car, people have asked 'Can you make a faster one?', and there has never been a shortage of madmen willing to try. The consequences of this search for outright speed saw Andy Green travelling across the salt flats in Thrust SSC at over 760mph, whilst in terms of street legal machinery the twin-engined Tiger T100 is amongst the fastest ever.

The day Colin Chapman penned the original Lotus 7 design is one which changed the world for small sports car manufacturers forever, and many cars have since been developed looking remarkably similar, but often with vastly differing levels of performance. When powered by two Kawasaki ZX9 900cc motorcycle engines, together putting out 304bhp, the Tiger T100 has been timed reaching 60mph from scratch in just 2.74 seconds and 100mph in 6.8 seconds, and all for just under £30,000. Top speed figures are not quoted as the 1960s inspired design is not aerodynamically efficient, and militates increasingly against it at higher speeds.

PORSCHE 930

◄ When a car such as the Porsche 911 has been going for such a long time, choosing one particular model from its evolution is not easy, but the model more brutal and recognisable than most is the 930, or 911 Turbo as it is sometimes (incorrectly) known.

Originally launched at the 1974 Paris Motor Show, it was one of the first cars to use a turbo, and it grew in performance as the years went by, without growing significantly in the handling department. During the madness of the 1980s, when people were getting rich overnight, the Porsche became one of the status symbols *de rigueur*, often bought by inexperienced young men armed with a huge bonus payment inversely proportional to their ability to handle the immense power of an extremely tail-happy wild beast.

A not inconsiderable number of 930s ended their road-careers very shortly after they'd left the showroom: performance figures of 0–60mph in less than 5 seconds and a top speed of 165mph demanded the sort of respect many of their *nouveau riche* owners were unable to afford the car, with all too predictable results.

VAUXHALL LOTUS CARLTON

▶ Whilst it would be both unkind and untrue to suggest that, throughout their history, Vauxhalls and high speed have been mutually exclusive, it would come as a considerable surprise for most people to discover that the world's fastest ever four-door saloon until very recently bore the familiar Griffin badge on its bonnet.

In 1990, GM's recently purchased Lotus Group set to work, turning the ordinary Carlton saloon into the ultimate fire-breathing Q-car with a 377bhp 3.6-litre, 24-valve, twin turbo straight-six engine, which a number of magazines tested at speeds of up to 178mph. This, however, does not fully depict the sheer grunt and power of the beast: it was capable of a sprint to 140mph from standstill in just 24 seconds. Just 800 examples were built, selling in the UK for £45,000, and today the survivors are widely respected and owned by loving collectors, who prize highly their Porsche-eating four-door saloons.

FERRARI ENZO

▼ The day after Italy's Ferrari F1 team clinched its fourth consecutive World Championship in 2003, the company launched the Enzo, its fastest ever road car, named after the company's founder.

Whilst arguably not the most beautiful Ferrari, its 6-litre V12 – which delivered a whopping 660bhp – ensured that it had the means traditionally employed by Ferraris to attract customers: sensational amounts of power available on demand. With a body made from carbon-fibre and aluminium honeycomb, it was both immensely strong and very light, whilst one aspect which differentiated the Enzo from many other supercars was the lack of a large rear spoiler, made redundant by superb under-body airflow management.

Only 399 were ever built, and sold almost immediately to buyers hooked on the notion of 0–60 sprint times of 3.6 seconds and a top speed of 220mph.

CHAPTER TWO

HOW EXTRAVAGANT!

ASTON MARTIN LAGONDA VIGNALE

▶ When Aston Martin unveiled their Lagonda Vignale concept car at the Geneva Salon of 1993, reaction, although mixed, was largely favourable. This was a taster of Ford's vision of what a 21st-century Aston Martin four-door limousine might look like, and was launched to gauge the public reaction to such a concept. It was built on a Lincoln chassis, was powered by a 4.6-litre V8, and clothed in retro-styled, art deco inspired bodywork designed by Moray Callum and constructed by Ghia of Turin.

'An Aston Martin combines three important elements: power, beauty and soul.' So says the official website, and the Lagonda Vignale most definitely conformed to this ethos. Its interior was unlike that of any other before or since, whilst its glorious coachwork was sensuous in every detail. Two examples were built, one of which was sold at auction in June 2002, realising $403,500 including buyer's premium.

FRAZER TICKFORD METRO

▼ One would not normally expect to find the humble Austin Metro in the pages of a chapter devoted to the upper reaches of the luxury car market, but the Frazer Tickford Metro of 1981 was no ordinary Metro. At £11,600, this was big money for a little car, whose only real mechanical improvement over its humbler brethren was the addition of a better carburettor which marginally improved the A series engine's output, giving 80bhp at the wheels.

It also gained swanky alloy wheels, half a herd of cows' hides covering virtually the entire interior, and an up-market hi-fi system. Of all the cars to pick for a makeover, the Austin Metro must have ranked among the least obvious, and whether all this extravagance of Connolly hide etc was worth the effort is a matter of opinion.

VGD BENTLEY SHOOTING BRAKE

◄ The Bentley Arnage is a timeless classic of a car, which year on year is improved almost imperceptibly. Its lines are so graceful that it is difficult to imagine how one could improve them … unless you are super-rich, already have a Bentley, but at the same time need something with a bit more luggage capacity.

For many people in such a situation, the solution would be quite straightforward: keep the Bentley and buy a Range Rover as well. Such a solution may seem sensible, but if it does not appeal an alternative exists. VGD (Von Genaddi Design, of Manitowoc, Wisconsin, USA) have arrived at what must surely be the ultimate compromise – a Bentley Shooting Brake (or Estate, in common parlance).

Naturally, when commissioning such a bespoke car, it can be as individual as the customer's wallet is large, so no standard list of features exists. However, such luxuries as full-length sunroof are available, along with the ultimate in-car entertainment system.

EXCALIBUR ROADSTER

◄ The Excalibur Roadster was an American interpretation of, or homage-paying exercise to, the graceful lines of the Mercedes 540K from 1936.

As one might expect, this car came fully equipped with everything that a wealthy American purchaser at the beginning of the 1980s (the decade of excess) might anticipate. Its ability to travel reasonable distances between fill-ups was guaranteed by a 30-gallon fuel tank, which was drained through a four-barrel carburettor into a 5-litre Chrysler V8 engine. Weighing more than four tons, this was more of a cruiser than the original 540K had been, but with extras such as cruise-control, air-conditioning, and even a powered dickey-seat, it made quite a statement, and was guaranteed to turn heads everywhere it went.

MERCEDES-BENZ CLS55 AMG

▼ The CLS is an entirely new concept in luxury motoring. Traditionally, luxury cars have been saloons, although of recent years a number of SUVs have muscled their way into this desirable corner of the marketplace. But now Mercedes-Benz have blended the sensuality of a coupé shape with the best of the saloon attributes to create a new and highly distinctive shape.

With the top-of-the-range £68,000 V8-powered CLS55 AMG, however, the shape is a mere distraction: this is a real bruiser of a car every bit as capable and arguably more attractive than the new BMW M5. Its limited top speed of 155mph is *de rigueur* in cars of this specification, but a 0–60mph sprint time of 4.7 seconds is most definitely impressive. Yet it is so much more than just a high-speed thrills machine, as its interior is a fabulously luxurious environment in which to travel, and here, also, the car raises the standard that other manufacturers will have to equal if they are to compete.

MOHS OSTENTATIENNE OPERA SEDAN

▲ Manufacturers are forever trying to make their designs different to their competitors', so that they will stand out in a crowded street. Very few have ever managed to achieve a design so completely unique, however, as the Mohs Ostentatienne Opera Sedan of 1968.

Its huge tyres, filled with nitrogen, were allegedly capable of 100,000 miles, whilst its single door at the rear was sold as a safety feature, brought about by the steel anti-intrusion beams running the length of the highly unconventional body. Inside, there was a refrigerator, the instrument panel had 24ct gold inlay in the walnut, there were Ming dynasty carpets on the floor, and illumination was achieved courtesy of hidden lighting. If the standard 304cu in V8 was deemed too miserly, a 549cu in V8 could be specified, and, thus specified, the car cost $25,600 before taxes or the addition of any further options.

Only one was ever built.

ROLLS-ROYCE PHANTOM

▼ When BMW took over stewardship of motoring's most prestigious name, the world wondered how the new owners from Munich would interpret and nurture the unique heritage that came with one of the world's most desired trademarks.

They need not have worried, for the Phantom, launched in January 2003, was everything that a Rolls-Royce should be, and arguably more than some of its recent predecessors had been. There are those who hold that since the Silver Shadow the cars lacked the size and sheer presence a proper Rolls-Royce should have: not so the Phantom. Powered by a 6.75-litre V12, superlatives are the norm when it comes to describing the car's attributes. Considerably more high-tech than many previous Royces had been at launch, the Phantom is built to the owner's personal specification, and is the paragon of both modernity and luxury: in every way, it is deserving of the moniker first accorded to its distant ancestor the Silver Ghost back in 1907: 'the finest motor-car in the world'.

ROBIN BN2

◀ Rising like a resin Phoenix after its demise resulting from Reliant's change of ownership, the Robin BN1 was launched on 12 July 2001. On the very same day, the BN2 version was announced, which was a very different beast from the 'resin-rockets' or 'plastic-pigs' of old. Whilst it still had three wheels and superficially looked similar, albeit rather more contemporary, this one came with electric windows, leather upholstery, and even a CD player all fitted as standard, for £10,000.

Even its paintwork was unique: in place of the dull primary colours such as beige, orange, or green, this one came with light reactive paint that changed colour according to the conditions. The idea of a funky, almost exciting Robin, with reasonable luxury and 80mpg, was most appealing, but bureaucracy soon stepped in, stopping production after just 50 units as the new car did not comply with certain DVLC regulations. Whilst trying to modify the car to meet these the money ran out, and the business was forced into voluntary liquidation.

MAYBACH EXELERO

▼ Since the esteemed name of Maybach was revived in 2002 to challenge Rolls-Royce's claim to build the world's finest motor-cars, it has been attached to limousines of previously undreamed levels of luxury.

In 2005, however, it also appeared on the bonnet of a one-off supercar, known as the Exelero, commissioned by German tyre manufacturer Fulda as a test-bed for its high performance tyres. High performance was most definitely available on demand from the aggressive-looking monster, with 700bhp developed from its bi-turbo V12 6-litre engine, giving a top speed of 218mph.

Whilst most of the car's appearance – the work of 24-year-old Frederik Burchhardt – is striking and highly pleasing, more work could possibly have improved the grille, which looks more like it belongs on a kit car than a hugely expensive machine built by one of the planet's most distinguished manufacturers.

VGD GTR

▲ Genaddi Design Group is a company of American Master Coachbuilders with almost 25 years' experience of tailoring cars to the exact whims of the wealthiest of clients. Their creations are startling, often interpreting and in some cases finishing the design of a car that the original manufacturer might have been too timid to complete.

A good example of this is the VGD GTR of 2004. This amazing creation has retained all the best qualities of the Bentley Continental GT on which it is based, but carries the design through to its natural conclusion by giving it a convertible steel roof. The lines of the car have been kept largely intact, although larger wheels and bulging wheel-arches lend it a more muscular air.

Ever since the Bentley was launched there have been questions over whether the company may build a convertible version one day: one look at the skilful work of the master craftsmen of the Genaddi Design Group should be enough to convince even the most timid of decision makers at Crewe that this is a car they should be offering.

CADILLAC V16

▼ The time taken to develop a car and bring it to market has occasionally meant that by the time it goes on sale, the market for it is no longer there. At the beginning of the 1990s Jaguar found themselves in this awkward spot with their £403,000 supercar, the XJ220, bringing it to market after the economic bubble that spurred them into making it had burst and there were no longer people around with that sort of money to blow on pointless cars.

Sixty years earlier it had been the turn of Cadillac to suffer this fate, as they had to launch their V16 model in 1930, just months after the Wall Street Crash had sent the world's markets into meltdown and precipitated the Great Depression. This was the world's first production V16, and at 7.4 litres developing 165bhp was a new benchmark. Naturally, the cars into which these engines went were opulent in the extreme, with many different body styles and options on offer.

VG AUTO MAYBACH CONVERTIBLE

◄ No one could suggest that the Maybach 57 is a car short of charisma or appeal, and yet for some it is not quite special enough. And for just such people, there is someone who can give it that extra little something: step forward Mark Gerisch, whose company, Genaddi Design Group, specialises in uprating exotica.

One would not normally turn to the Maybach 57 as an example of a car that is likely to look better without its roof, and yet the end result is truly stunning. With the hood up, it retains all the elegance of the saloon; but with the hood down, it looks entirely different. Here is a car so luxurious that it costs £243,780 in standard form: the conversion work adds a further £120,000 to that price. It is a car for which new superlatives must be invented.

RENAULT VEL SATIS

► Car designers can be an insecure bunch of people. The pressure to get it right first time and make the next model a huge success for the manufacturer is immense, and the cost of failure can be most damaging to fragile egos. Small surprise, then, that by most people's judgement most cars look the same. Virtually no one is prepared to take the risk of going off on a tangent, however strongly they may believe in their design. Ask BMW's designer Chris Bangle about the consequences of trying to be different: X Coupé, anyone?

The Renault Vel Satis, however, is one car that has tried to change our expectations of a luxury vehicle. It stands 13cm higher than the average car for its class, and while some intensely dislike its styling, to others it is the epitome of French chic. In Initiale trim it comes loaded with every conceivable gadget, including xenon headlights, an interior that feels like a Bang & Olufsen design, heated windscreen washers, satnav, electro-chrome door-mirrors, etc …

The car-buying public remain unconvinced, however, and even in the intensely patriotic French home market a Vel Satis is a depressingly rare sight.

BENTLEY AZURE

◄ The Bentley Azure, launched at the Geneva Motor Show on 7 March 1995, is a modern interpretation of the classic Grand Tourer: supremely elegant, effortlessly powerful, dignified, proud, and exquisitely luxurious.

Its graceful lines – a development of the successful Continental R – were penned by the draftsmen at Pininfarina, while its coachwork was lovingly put together by the craftsmen at Mulliner Park Ward. Its 6.75-litre V8 gave it a highly respectable top speed of 150mph, which can be experienced with the hood either up or down without causing any discomfort to the occupants if it was lowered.

Such luxury and perfection does not come cheap, however, and at launch the Azure's price was £182,978 before taxes.

JAGUAR R-COUPÉ

▶ Few companies have their design studies fussed and picked-over by the media more than Jaguar, so when they launched the R-Coupé at the 2002 New York International Auto Show it was immediately taken seriously as a signal of intent regarding the Coventry firm's future designs.

Designed by Ian Callum, it is in the classic Gran Tourismo style, with an art deco influenced interior of immense quality and luxury. The traditional elements of Jaguar interiors, wood and leather, are present in abundance in the R-Coupé's cabin, used in classy and modern ways to accentuate the futuristic thinking behind the car's design philosophy. Externally, LED front fog lights and indicators, 21in alloy wheels, and solid silver badging – including subtle Union Jack emblems in the side vents – all contribute to a most desirable car that the world is still waiting for the chance to buy.

ZIMMER GOLDEN SPIRIT

▼ In 1978, an American called Paul Zimmer bought an Excalibur as a fun car, but was not greatly impressed. In a Ferruccio Lamborghini moment of 'I can do better than this ...', the Zimmer Motor Car Company was born. Whilst Zimmer is a name that many people outside the USA may never have heard of in the context of cars, this is a shame, as its own website describes it as 'the most awesome automobile in the world', and, in styling terms alone, this may not be that far from the truth.

A huge car, the Golden Spirit is based on the Lincoln Town Car, and uses many of its mechanical components. Its styling combines the flowing lines of a mid-1930s Duesenberg with the modern passenger cell of an American limousine. Unlikely as it may seem the mix works, and the resulting car, whilst definitely unusual, is not the hideous pastiche one might expect. It is a hand-built machine (a mere 1,400 have been built to date), and only 15–20 are constructed per year. They are built to order, and, as one would expect of such a car, whose appearance makes it most suited to Las Vegas or Hollywood, luxury fittings abound.

STATE BENTLEY

◄ Before 2002, the British Royal family had never used a Bentley as an official state car, but the Crewe-based firm, fresh from its divorce from Rolls-Royce (which had hitherto supplied the Queen with four state limousines), presented her with a £10 million one-off car to celebrate her Golden Jubilee. The official hand-over took place on 29 May 2002, and it was then pressed into a hectic schedule of engagements around the country.

Designed with input from the Queen, Prince Philip, and the Head Chauffeur, the 20ft, 3.4-tonne limousine is powered by a 400bhp version of the venerable 6.75-litre V8 as used in the Arnage and many previous Rolls-Royce and Bentley cars. Inside the huge vehicle, the rear seats are upholstered in Hield Lambswool Sateen Cloth, while the rest of the seats are covered in light grey Connolly hide. Whilst fuel costs are not in themselves a huge concern for the royal family, the car is capable of running on LPG, for ecological reasons. At the Queen's request, electronic gadgets have been kept to a minimum.

It is scheduled to stay in service until 2027.

PEUGEOT 607 PALADINE

▲ Launched at the Geneva Motor Show 2000, the Peugeot 607 Paladine appeared to be a cross between a standard 607, a stretched limousine, and a 206 CC. Here was an attempt to build a super-stretched limousine fit for a French president, with all the benefits of open-top motoring for special cavalcades as and when weather and security considerations would allow.

Now measuring over 5m, the V6, 3-litre Paladine sat on 18in alloy wheels, shod in Michelin PAX anti-puncture tyres, whilst inside as much luxury as it was practical to fit had been installed, including a library section, refrigerated bar, sophisticated stereo system, climate control which can alter for different parts of the cabin, reclining rear seats, electrically powered headrests, and adjustable foot rests, whilst the Hermes-trimmed interior came in 'Clemence' – a sapphire blue calf leather – and a unique H-patterned cloth woven in cotton and silk.

MAYBACH 62

◄ When the world's oldest car manufacturer, Mercedes-Benz, lost out in the first round to Volkswagen and BMW in the battle to buy the world's most prestigious manufacturer, Rolls-Royce, there must have been some sorely bruised egos in Stuttgart. So much did it hurt that, within a very short space of time indeed, M-B announced that *they* were going to build the world's finest car, not Rolls-Royce, and it would be called a Maybach.

The car they built and finally launched in 2002 was a massively impressive beast, even if it did look uncomfortably like an overgrown Mercedes-Benz, boasting phenomenal amounts of technology, gadgetry, marquetry, leather, and a general ambience of luxury that had never been previously seen crammed into one car. Powered by a 12-cylinder behemoth of an engine boasting two turbos, 550bhp, and a 0–60 sprint of 5.4 seconds without uttering more than the most polite of murmurs, it is available in two sizes, the 57 and 62, where these figures refer to the wheelbase.

Among the luxuries available for specification by the owner are such innovations as electro-transparent panels in the roof, DVD, and a 600w stereo system. In fact, so long is the list of options that it is a test of the decision-making qualities of the owner: an owner who is most unlikely ever actually to sit behind the steering wheel.

The difference between the Maybach and the Rolls-Royce Phantom is that the Rolls-Royce is a car the owner may wish to drive, whilst the Maybach is more of a chauffeur-driven car, where the greatest luxuries are to be found in seats other than the driver's.

BUGATTI ROYALE

▼ The Bugatti Royale – or, to give it its more mundane name, the Bugatti Type 41 – was a huge machine in every conceivable way. Its 12.8-litre straight-eight overhead cam engine gave the 5,600lb leviathan a top speed of 100mph, from 275bhp.

When originally conceived it was aimed at royalty, but no royal or head of state ever bought one. Only six were built between 1927 and 1933, three of which saw service with the Bugatti family themselves. When new, they cost more than three times the price of a Rolls-Royce Phantom II, giving them the further distinction of being the most expensive road-car ever put into production. All six survive to this day, and on the rare occasions that they come up for sale they continue this tradition of commanding extraordinarily high prices.

CHAPTER THREE

WHAT WERE THEY

GOLD LABEL

▼ Sounding more like a packet of cigarettes than a car, the Gold Label, based on the mechanicals of the Bentley Turbo, was the handiwork of the late Robert Jankel, mastermind behind Panther cars, including the six-wheeled Panther Six.

Up until the Second World War (and in some cases even a decade or so after it), wealthy purchasers of cars such as Rolls-Royces and Bentleys would buy their vehicles in chassis form and then have the coachbuilder of their choice manufacture a body to their own tastes. Appearing in the mid-1990s, the Gold Label was a late, if not entirely successful, rebirth of this by now long dead tradition.

Were it not for the stylised and heavily sloping interpretation of a Bentley grille, there would be little on the surface to suggest that this was anything other than a mid-range American convertible. And yet, underneath the unsuccessful 'Knight-Rider meets Jeeves and Wooster' appearance there lurked Crewe's finest oily bits, delivering sub 5-second 0–60 sprint times and a top speed in excess of 150mph.

Very few were ever sold.

PORSCHE CAYENNE

▶ Throughout the 1990s, the SUV enjoyed a constant growth in popularity, especially in the all-important US market. Manufacturers who had built their reputations, and often their entire business plans, around the executive sector of the market watched this growing phenomenon and planned accordingly. One company that felt the need to get a piece of this action was Porsche, whose entire history hitherto had been built around fast cars and racetracks.

The Cayenne is the car they launched in November 2002 to stake a claim in the SUV corner of the marketplace, and a very strange beast it is. Mindful of their heritage, Porsche made sure that not only did it go extremely quickly (in 'Turbo' trim, 0–60 in 5.6 seconds and a top speed of 165mph), but that from certain angles there was more than a passing resemblance to the real sports cars with which they are more normally associated.

Pretty, however, it is not. Unnecessarily expensive, the ability to mix ultra high speeds with the ability to go off-road is the answer to a question that no one asked – especially when the ugly behemoth that is the Porsche Cayenne is that answer.

THINKING OF?

BMW X COUPÉ

▼ BMW drivers, on the whole, know what they like, and, being innately conservative, they like to watch product from the Munich-based company evolve along safe, unchallenging lines.

One thing they don't like, and of which they were most vocal in expressing their disgust, was the X coupé, first shown in 2001. Designer Chris Bangle, who had previously designed the Fiat Turbo coupé before joining BMW, felt that BMW design was something that needed a shake-up to take it into the new century, and the X coupé was an early attempt at leading the BMW faithful down his chosen path. Clothed in aluminium bodywork, straight lines were nowhere to be seen, and the talk was of 'tension' across the panels, and new design language.

The tension was not long in coming, however, as previously loyal BMW owners erupted in columns of vitriol in the letters pages of their favourite car magazines, and Mr Bangle became the subject of some language of a rather more earthy nature than the flowery prose he used to describe this 'enfant horrible'.

The mistake was soon acknowledged, however, and the PR disaster quickly disappeared, never to be mentioned again in polite society.

HABIB SITARA

▶ Whilst it is easy to sneer at the cars coming from the developing world, 2004's Habib Sitara is by any standards a crude machine.

Aimed at the same market Henry Ford was originally keen to adopt, ie those who were unable to afford a car, the Sitara is little more than a motorised platform, and even the motor is endowed with just 170cc. Its proud makers, however, point to such concessions to safety as seatbelts all round, a roll-bar and handlebars readily to hand to enable the occupants to hang on in case the upper limits of its admittedly poor performance are being explored by a carefree driver. Soft padding has been added at crucial points to aid both safety and comfort.

Ideal for its native territory of Pakistan, the Habib Sitara is a rough but thoroughly rugged machine, and may, like its forebears such as the Citroën 2CV, appeal to its home market: exports seem less likely.

MOHS SAFARIKAR

▲ The spelling of this most bizarre machine is probably the least unusual feature of a car that comprehensively ignored virtually every convention of car building. Allegedly, it was designed as a luxury off-roader to go hunting in.

Available in penny numbers between 1972 and 1975, its body was made from aluminium, padded with Naugahyde, and was attached to a chassis from an International Harvester 2 truck. The large grille at the front was the first sign of trouble ahead in the taste department, whilst further back huge sliding doors and a retractable roof further confounded the spectator. Most unusual of all was its ability to accommodate eight passengers and the rear seat's ability to transform into a double bed.

Its price of $14,500 may have been instrumental in dissuading potential customers from stepping forward, but its sheer daftness is more likely to have been the real reason.

BUGATTI EB110

▲ If every car has a song, then the perhaps not too politically-correct late 1970s hit *Nice legs, shame about the face* by the Monks would have to be the song for the 1994 Bugatti EB110. Its legs, in the form of a 3.5-litre V12, 60-valve engine, which in 'Super Sport' tune delivered 610bhp, took it via a sophisticated four-wheel-drive system to 60mph in 3.3 seconds and carried on to the far side of 200mph; but its face – well, its entire body – was wincingly ugly.

Super fast, super luxury is always a heady combination, and likely to attract punters, but the Marcello Gandini designed body – hard to believe he also designed such beauties as the Lamborghini Countach and Lancia Stratos – was enough to put off all but the most hardened performance junkies. Michael Schumacher had one, and apparently liked it.

TOYOTA YARIS VERSO

▼ Strange but true: even the world's second largest motor manufacturer is capable of the occasional blind spot when it comes to signing off the metal-and-four-wheels equivalent of Quasimodo. No one can deny that the Toyota Yaris is a perfectly capable car, but one cannot but wonder if the entire Taste and Good Looks Department were off on a long weekend break when the plans for the Verso version of January 2000 came up for scrutiny prior to being passed for production and a presence on the world's roads.

Laying aside the conventions of good manners, nothing on this carbuncle can be truly described as appealing. If a contest were to be organised to find the world's most hideous mistake of motoring design, the Yaris Verso would almost certainly be guaranteed a place in the final.

FORD SCORPIO

▶ In 1994, the Ford Motor Company heavily re-worked its ageing Granada Scorpio. Mechanically it was much improved: it drove better, the interior was luxurious, and it was generally a nice car to be in. In order to experience this feeling, however, one had first to overcome the mixture of shock, mirth, ridicule, and sheer disbelief when looking at the startling exterior.

Its predecessor had been a quiet, dignified, and unassuming design. The new car, however, was so comprehensively and undisputedly ugly that many were left wondering if this was all a big joke, or if, perhaps, the disguises manufacturers use to protect the secrecy of their forthcoming new cars had been inadvertently left on. Indeed, the highly respected *Car* magazine featured it on their front cover following its launch and asked in bold letters, 'Whodunit?' The article inside went in search of the perpetrators of this most baffling makeover.

FIAT MULTIPLA

▼ When the first spy-shots of the Multipla prototype appeared in the pages of the world's motoring press, no one really believed that this strange form with lights in weird places and daft blobby appearance, complete with Fisher Price inspired interior, would ever make it into production without serious modification from the Sensible Department. And yet, by some quirk of history as yet unexplained, Fiat — one of the world's most senior motor manufacturers — launched this most abstract of forms on the almost completely unprepared world. It was subsequently rated No. 4 of the world's most ugly vehicles in a Channel 4 TV poll in the UK.

While some motoring journalists, and many larger families, praised its sixth seat (located in the front between driver and passenger) and much besides, most observers struggled to prevent their jaws from scraping the pavements as they saw the first examples of this most unorthodox form drive by in the summer of 1999.

The second generation is significantly more conservative than the original: perhaps the most significant admission that the original had been a little too extreme for most customers' tastes.

PONTIAC AZTEK

▲ Good taste and good looks are highly contentious concepts and can cause much debate and disagreement. One name, however, which kept coming up on an Internet forum debating which is the most ugly car currently on sale, was the Pontiac Aztek, released in 2001.

The design is most definitely challenging, and appears to be the work of two designers who were simultaneously working to different briefs. The upper half of the body appears top be the work of the designer who thought he was working on a family saloon, whilst the lower half of the car looks like the work of someone who felt that a rugged 4x4 was his brief. One can imagine that at some stage, perhaps over a coffee and cigarette break late in the design process, they discovered this lack of unity of thought, and resolved the issue by combining the two designs. Even the specifications on offer tend to support this theory, with the choice of front-wheel drive or 4x4.

Whilst Pontiac will doubtless sell many Azteks, the democratic process of Internet forum chat has put the car in this chapter.

COMMUTER CARS TANGO

◄ Some cars are so bizarre in appearance that a second look has to be taken, as if to make doubly sure one's eyes are working properly. One such car is 2004's Tango, modern electric city car from America, a country not normally associated with small, nippy, economical cars.

Viewed side-on, its sleek bodywork looks not unlike a Smart car, with the passenger sitting tandem-style behind the driver. When viewed head-on, however, it is uniquely slender and at its most bizarre. Its designers set out to surprise onlookers further by giving it startling performance. It must surely rate amongst the all-time fastest of electric cars, with a 0–60mph time of 4 seconds and a top speed of a barely believable 120mph.

NEVCO GIZMO

▶ The Nevco Gizmo is an amazing machine, resembling, from the front at least, a Dyson carpet cleaner. It is a 21st-century electric vehicle capable of speeds of up to 40mph, whilst costing just one penny per mile in running costs. Its full running costs actually equate to nearer 20p per mile, but it is nevertheless an amazingly cheap and Earth-friendly means of transport.

Advertised as the car 'Big enough to scare OPEC' and the car that 'Fits into places other cars can't. Like the ecosystem', the Nevco Gizmo is a thoroughly modern, if rather quirky, machine, extreme not only in appearance but also in its claims and aims.

ALFA ROMEO ARNA

▼ Imagine receiving an invitation to the wedding of Johnny Vegas and Claudia Schiffer: you'd probably rub your eyes, assume it's a practical joke, and throw it in the bin. Now try transposing this scenario into a marriage of car company offspring, and the result would be the Alfa Romeo Arna.

The Arna was a uniquely awful blend of Japanese styling (Nissan Cherry) and unreliable Italian electrics and poor build quality from Alfa Romeo, rescued only in part by the inclusion of an Alfasud engine and rear suspension by way of dowry.

Launched in 1983 and built at an entirely new factory at Pratola Serra, near Naples, it was available in three engine sizes, ranging from 1,200cc to 1,500cc, with the largest engine putting out 95bhp. For all the most obvious and predictable reasons, the project died within three years of launch.

LAMBORGHINI LM002

◄ The LM002, launched by Lamborghini in 1986, was such an extreme machine it is hard to equate it with the rest of the company's products. A total of just 301 of these monsters was built, powered by a V12 5.2-litre 48-valve engine (as used in the Countach), which developed a whopping 455bhp and delivered a top speed of 116mph. Later examples used even larger engines, including a 7.3-litre version.

Everything about the LM002 was extreme. Weighing in at 3,100kg, it stood 1.9m high, 2m wide, and 4.9m long. With such weight to move around it seemed wise to give it a large fuel tank, and 290 litres was judged to be adequate. Most cars were destined for the Middle East, where fuel costs are simply not relevant, and a number of them saw service in the Saudi Arabian army, while the civilian models were equipped with every luxury imaginable.

FORD EDSEL

▼ 'Once you've seen it, you'll never forget it.' So ran the advertising strapline for the infamous Edsel. No chapter on car design faux pas would be complete without mentioning the most famous carbuncle of all. Launched in 1957, it came with the latest in gizmos, including auto transmission controlled from buttons on the steering wheel boss.

Launch day, called 'E Day', was 4 September 1957, and followed months of teaser advertising which resulted in 2.5 million Americans flocking to see the new car in Ford showrooms across the United States. What they saw, however, was not the graceful lines of a new generation of dream cars, but a hideous monstrosity.

Unsurprisingly, very few sold, partly due to a recession, but mainly due to the car's disastrous appearance. Within three years the Edsel division was closed, after two facelifts failed to convince most would-be punters to buy one.

VEXEL QUOVIS

▲ The Vexel Quovis is a car with a noble purpose: that of providing full motoring ability for those in wheelchairs. This does not, however, mean that it needs to look quite as odd as it does, and its appearance can only be described as extremely unusual, if not quirky.

Entry is from the rear, which opens at the press of a button on the key fob, and once inside everything is automatic. It is capable of 100mpg, and being a single-seater it is not available in either left- or right-hand drive. It is therefore well suited to any market around the world.

AURORA

► Catholic priests do not, as a rule, good car designers make, and American Fr Alfredo Juliano proved no exception. Arguably, his creation – the Aurora safety car of 1957 – was the ugliest car ever built.

It would appear that the good priest's caring nature extended beyond that of his parish, as he incorporated a number of safety features into his car, including seat belts, foam-filled bumpers mounted on ram-rods, roll-over bars built into its 'astrodome roof', and even a telescopic steering column. Its monstrous fibreglass bodywork featured extravagant swirls down the sides giving the car the appearance of being driven everywhere in reverse. Its bulbous perspex windscreen was supposed to remove the need for wipers, but replicating it gave the car's restorer, Andy Saunders, more headaches than any other aspect of this one-off monstrosity.

DEAUVILLE CANJITO

▶ The Citroën 2CV, covered elsewhere in this book, was a marvellous machine which appealed to many different types. Whilst indisputably rugged, many examples' lives were ended prematurely due to terminal rust. Over the years, many kits have been launched using the mechanicals from 2CVs that have fallen victim to rust, and 2004's Deauville Canjito is one of the more recent.

Its stark, almost butch plastic bodywork sits on top of the Citroën's donor chassis, supported by a substantial steel superstructure which also gives the open-topped car roll-over hoops for added safety. Whilst 2CV enthusiasts would stop short of calling the new look an improvement, there are improvements under the bonnet which all will welcome. These include electronic ignition, uprated electrics, a new exhaust system, and halogen headlights.

Its looks might suggest it would be more at home in the Transvaal than in Surrey, but as a fun car, at less than £6,500 including the cost of the donor vehicle, this unusual curiosity is an interesting visual punctuation mark in the sea of modern automotive blandness.

CHEVROLET CORVAIR

▲ The 1960 Chevrolet Corvair was not just a bad car in terms of its safety record and the fact that $4 worth of anti-roll bars could have fixed its treacherous suspension; it also just looked plain bad.

The era of excessive fins was drawing to a close, and car design in America was looking for a new direction. The Corvair was certainly radically different from previous offerings, with its 2.3-litre flat 6, air-cooled engine placed at the rear of the unitary-construction body, imitating VW and – more importantly for sales purposes – Porsche. However, its dangerously wayward handling resulting from the lack of anti-roll bars, and a pronounced tendency to understeer if owners neglected to monitor carefully the need for 15psi in the front tyres and 26psi in the rear, were famously pointed out by Ralph Nader in his book *Unsafe at any Speed*, and the car never recovered its reputation thereafter.

GEM E825/4

◄ Not so much a name, more a prisoner number, the E825/4 is a 21st-century electric vehicle of bewildering appearance, which in many ways resembles what one would imagine a Fiat Multipla would look like without any of its body panels attached.

GEM, or Global Electric Motorcars, is a division of DaimlerChrysler, and is based in Fargo, North Dakota. It makes a variety of electric vehicles, and these are designed, most surprisingly, for use on the road, rather than the golf course where one might perhaps expect to find such an unorthodox machine as the E825/4. Its top speed is governed to a none-too-frightening 25mph, and with careful driving it should cover up to 30 miles on a single charge.

SSANG YONG RODIUS

▶ The Ssang Yong Rodius is guilty of the same mistake as the Pontiac Aztek inasmuch as it appears to be two cars compressed into one, but the Rodius has been met with such an outcry in the motoring press, that its title of the Ugliest Car currently on sale seems likely to go unchallenged.

Whilst it has some virtues, principal among which are the interior space and Mercedes-Benz engines and running gear, there is little else to recommend the car, and Angus Fitton, reviewing it for *Car* magazine in September 2005, summed it up succinctly, if somewhat cruelly, by saying 'It's hard to believe, but it's almost as bad as it looks.'

CREE SAM

▶ The SAM is a startling three-wheeled machine, which, unusually, is powered by electricity. Its top speed of just over 50mph, whilst perhaps not unexpected given its power source, is nevertheless disappointing given its waspish shape. This shape, with its occupants seated in tandem formation, is further sexed-up by its double gullwing doors, and in matt black the contraption looks more menacing than its top speed can ever hope to live up to.

Considering its strong visual appeal, green credentials, and Swiss nationality, it is surprising that the project has so far been unable to attract sufficient backing to go into full production.

McQUAY-NORRIS STREAMLINER

◄ To a greater or lesser extent, streamlining has been a feature of car design from very early in its history. A relatively early attempt at reducing aerodynamic drag (and attracting attention for the company's more central activities) was the bizarre-looking McQuay-Norris Streamliner of 1934.

Based on the chassis and running gear of a Ford V8, the bodywork of steel and aluminium was attached to a wooden frame and had Plexiglas windows. They were built to be driven by sales representatives selling McQuay-Norris engine components, but served a second purpose as test-beds for the various components made by the company. This explains the profusion of dials and instruments inside the cramped cabin.

A total of just six were built, of which two are known to survive.

ALFA ROMEO RZ

▼ Alfa Romeo have built some remarkable machinery during their long history, often clothed in truly inspired coachwork. The SZ from 1989, however, did not belong in this exclusive club. In essence it was a heavily reworked Alfa 75, with the most unappealing bodywork imaginable made from Modar, a composite material. Amazingly, given its blunt, 'inspired by a house-brick' styling, it had a drag co-efficient of 0.30, and this enabled its 210bhp V6 3-litre engine to deliver a very respectable top speed of just over 150mph.

Production of a little over 1,200 examples, including the SZ coupé, was carried out by the renowned coachbuilder Zagato, and, perhaps due to the limited number, and the fact that this was the 1980s, it was regarded with much greater esteem than its Emperor's New Clothes appearance deserved.

CITROËN AMI 6

◄ At the beginning of the 1960s, the famously unorthodox French manufacturer Citroën launched the Ami 6 as a halfway house between the cheap-and-cheerful 2CV and the considerably more expensive DS19. It had four doors, four seats, and was capable of carrying much more luggage than the 2CV, but its styling could not be said to be to everyone's tastes.

To call it ugly would not really be a sufficient description of this uniquely quirky design, with its reverse-raked rear windscreen and decidedly challenging frontal aspect. If the appearance alone were not enough to dissuade most sane people from wanting one, its meagre 602cc engine ensured that performance could not be relied upon to make full amends for the offence caused by the designer's pen. This was a rare example of French non-chic.

ONE DAY, ALL CARS

CITROËN DS

▶ The DS (pronounced Day-Esse in French, which means 'goddess'), was Citroën's first entirely new design after the Second World War, and was launched in 1955, replacing the 11CV. It may have been a long time in coming, but when it arrived it caused a huge stir, so modern and mould-breaking was it.

Apart from its uniquely slippery shape, it had a roomy interior, front-wheel-drive, power-operated self-levelling hydro-pneumatic suspension, hydraulic gear-change, power brakes, power steering, and the ability to adjust the car's ride height. All of this highly complex technology made considerable demands on the engines of the early cars, which were enlarged in later versions, and more gadgets such as steering-linked swivelling headlights (which illuminated the bend around which the car was turning) were added as the DS went through its 20-year life-cycle.

Even when it was finally replaced with the CX in 1975, the DS was still considered a modern and highly complex machine, and it is now collected by devotees of the marque.

ALFA ROMEO DISCO VOLANTE

▼ Named Disco Volante – Italian for 'flying saucer' – because its slippery shape was very science fiction, and flying saucers were highly newsworthy in 1952 (the year of its launch), this was a car built for racing. Its 3.5-litre, in-line six-cylinder engine developed a very useful 260bhp and a top speed of approximately 150mph.

This would have been enough to assure the car of victory in many of the races it entered, but unfortunately the car's designers (along with everybody else, to be fair) had only a fundamental knowledge of the exacting science of aerodynamics, and the body, whilst slippery and therefore not wasteful of energy in penetrating the air through which it was trying to race, generated too much lift, which made the Disco Volante something of a handful to drive at speed.

Only four were ever built, including one coupé.

MIGHT BE BUILT LIKE THIS ...

DYNAVIA

◄ The latter years of the Second World War saw many designers secretly working on projects that they intended to pursue once the conflict was over. One such man was Frenchman Louis Bionier, who was working for Panhard.

Studying the way birds fly, and the slippery efficiency of fish bodies, he worked on a model he called Dynavia, and once peace was restored he set about turning his aerodynamic shape into a full-size prototype car, which was first shown to the public at the Paris Salon in 1948. Its twin-cylinder, air-cooled 610cc engine was frugal, and yet was able to deliver a top speed of over 80mph whilst sipping its way through a gallon of fuel every 57 miles. Its extreme shape, however, ensured it never entered production, although many elements of this futuristic car saw production in subsequent Panhard models. Happily, the car still exists today, and is on display at the Schlumpf museum in Mulhouse.

BRUBAKER BOX

▶ Curtis Brubaker had a moment of inspiration one day in the late 1960s at Newport Beach, Southern California, when, noticing the large numbers of surfers using VW vans, he decided to design something equally usable but even cooler. The end result was the Brubaker Box. This in itself may not be that remarkable, were it not for the fact that it is credited with being the original inspiration for the people carriers that now populate the world's roads.

To call it a box was either unkind or unnecessarily modest, as although it was essentially a single-box design it was super cool and very much of its time, especially when fitted with the must-have Wolfrace wheels that were *de rigueur* amongst custom cars of the period. Brubaker wanted to sell it as a complete car, with a price tag of $3,995, but buying the components from VW – who were worried about liability issues – proved difficult, and so they were sold for a short while as kits. The efforts to try and persuade VW, however, had taken their toll, and not many vehicles were sold before bankruptcy finished the project: its legacy, however, lives on in countless driveways around the world.

AUDI QUATTRO

▶ Milestones in the history of motoring are defining moments, and the cars that bear the title invariably turn the industry's thinking on its head. The Ford Model T was a milestone, as were the VW Beetle, the Citroën DS, and the 1959 Mini. To this elite club a new member was admitted at the beginning of the 1980s, when Audi engineers showed the world how four-wheel-drive had uses beyond ensuring farmers could get around muddy fields.

The Audi Quattro was a fabulous car: it looked right, and with a top speed of 137mph (0–60 in 6.7 seconds) from its five-cylinder 2.2-litre engine, it went pretty well too. But what marked it out as a car above the rest was the way it could keep on delivering its power on road surfaces that had drivers of other cars backing off, or sliding off. Perhaps nowhere was this more vividly displayed than in rallying, where the new car – driven by such legends as Michel Mouton and Hannu Mikkola – swept all before it, and rewrote the rule-book on what was needed to win.

ASTON MARTIN BULLDOG

▶▶ Associating the title Bulldog with the quintessentially British name of Aston Martin was an undeniably good idea for gaining press attention, especially when you wanted them to look at something so futuristic that explaining its shape and function to an audience accustomed to somewhat more Olde Worlde offerings from Aston Martin was never going to be easy.

The William Towns-penned Bulldog was a concept shown at a number of motor shows during 1980, and it represented not only the company's aspirations, but also aimed to show to the likes of Ferrari that the Brits were able to match their offerings with sophisticated and high-tech designs of their own. A fully developed, road-going version was produced which was capable of speeds up to 180mph, with its traditional Aston Martin V8 mounted amidships behind the driver, who gained access to the most un-Aston-like machine through gullwing doors.

Fortunately, this playground posturing went no further than the one example, which still exists, and Aston Martin went back to building cars that were actually pleasant to look at, and deeply desirable, rather than anonymous wedge-shapes the like of which were later to inspire the true horrors of the De Lorean.

DELAHAYE T135M

▲ For such a staggeringly beautiful car, one cannot but feel slightly cheated by the paucity of imagination when it came to giving it a name. T135M sounds more like a part number than a fitting name for one of the most elegant cars from the 1930s, if not of all time.

The coachwork on this example was by Figoni and Falaschi, and it sat on top of a chassis of considerable modernity and ability derived from the firm's involvement in grand prix racing. Power came from a 3.5-litre in-line six-cylinder overhead-valve engine, which gave 160bhp and a top speed of 110mph.

In much the same way as in modern times Ferrari road cars are bought by the rich and famous, keen to bask in the glories of the F1 team, owners of Delahayes such as the T135M bought their cars both for the glamour of the grand prix victories and to satisfy their desire to own the zenith of automotive art.

HONDA KIWAMI

▼ Not all concept cars have to be essentially daft visions of a distant future, promising the unachievable before being wheeled off to a big store never to be seen again. The Honda Kiwami (which is Japanese for 'ultimate'), was first shown at the Tokyo Motor Show in 2003, and is a tasteful marriage of 21st-century fuel cell technology with minimalist architecture, producing a shape which is pleasant to see and a car that is kind to the environment.

This, however, is no dull eco-car. Its performance improves on earlier fuel-cell cars with the very latest technology, and with a low centre of gravity its handling is said to be exemplary, whilst inside all is luxury and refinement.

CHEVROLET SUBURBAN ½-TON LT

▲ America is a huge country, and some of its vehicles are incredibly large to match. One such behemoth is the Chevrolet Suburban, which in its largest and most lavish form – the ½-ton LT equipped with the 8100 Vortec V8 engine – is a machine that simply cannot fail to impress.

Everything about this car is built to extremes, from its size to its engine that only needs new spark plugs every 100,000 miles, and the coolant, which has a further 50 per cent lifespan. Its brakes have Hydro-Boost power assistance, whilst all four wheels are involved in the task of steering. Up to nine Americans can travel at any one time in this super-SUV, entertained by satellite radio or on-board DVD entertainment systems, whilst prices for a fully specced-up model can reach well over $55,000. When comparisons between earning power and car prices are made, this makes the Suburban a lot of car for the money.

BRISTOL FIGHTER

▶ Almost £230,000 is an awful lot to pay for a new car, but then, the Bristol Fighter, the first entirely new car from Bristol for 45 years, is mighty quick, with genuine exclusivity coming very much as part of the package.

Powered by an 8-litre V10 engine which delivers 525bhp, this sleek monster has a top speed of 210mph. It is one of very few cars ever to have been designed with aerodynamics a higher consideration than anything else, and although the performance is of true supercar stature this has not been achieved at the expense of luxury, which has long been an essential element of Bristol cars.

Precise numbers of Fighters built in any year since its 2003 launch are impossible to obtain, but so small is the output of the Filton factory that the likelihood of actually seeing a Fighter on the road is extremely small, which must be a source of comfort to the owners of slightly more common supercars unable to match its performance or exclusivity.

FIAT ECOBASIC

▼ Just occasionally a car, usually a concept, is wheeled out in public and one is left wondering if it is all some kind of practical joke. Surely they can't be *serious*?

One such car that, if nothing else, made the Fiat Multipla seem almost restrained and good-looking, was the Fiat Ecobasic of 2000. No adequate explanation was given for the car's appearance, although a low cd of just 0.28 was offered as some sort of apology, which helped the 61bhp 1.2-litre diesel engine (it doesn't get any better, does it?) reach 60mph in a soporific 13 seconds, and achieve 100mph and nearly 100mpg.

The minimalist approach to the design of the exterior, whereby apparently the least possible effort was expended on arriving at the car's shape, was carried over to the interior also, where the 'basic' part of the car's name suddenly explained itself.

Had the Ecobasic been designed by a kindergarten pupil no one would have batted an eyelid, but as a serious attempt at predicting the way future cars may look, one can only hope they were 100 per cent wrong.

COVINI C6W

▼ Designing a car is a complex process, but it can be made easier if one is prepared to take certain shortcuts. Principal among these is to not question certain ground rules that tend to govern the way (nearly) all cars are built. One such rule states that a car shall have four wheels, with the front pair doing the steering and most of the braking.

One company who have disregarded this rule are Covini from Italy, the home of supercars, and the result is the C6W, a 185mph supercar powered by a 4.2-litre V8 and steered by the front four of its six wheels. Whilst adding a second pair of tyres to the front of the car is hard to justify on aesthetic grounds, or higher tyre bills, it gives the car added steering stability plus, most crucially, considerably greater braking abilities.

Its extra pair of wheels are natural headline-grabbers, which is in some ways a shame, as its bodywork is startling and highly pleasing to behold, with features such as the vertically opening scissor doors and rear-mounted engine.

Production is unlikely.

ALFA ROMEO 6C 2500

◄ It is rumoured that whenever an Alfa Romeo passed by Henry Ford, he tipped his hat in salute. Had he lived to see the likes of the Arna, an Alfa engine in a Nissan body, he may well have stopped the habit, but in his day Alfa Romeo made some sensational cars, and, to be fair to them, although they don't always, they still can.

Just before the outbreak of the Second World War they began the manufacture of the 6C 2500, and after the war some of the surviving chassis were fitted with new bodywork, such as this example from 1948, whose stunning coachwork is believed to be the work of the Paris-based Saoutchik firm. Its racy looks were matched by a sporty performance from its six-cylinder engine, which gave a top speed of over 120mph.

RENAULT SPORT SPIDER

▼ For a company with such a long history, Renault is still remarkably young in its outlook, and is proud of its innovative reputation. Many of its cars seem almost deliberately provocative, and one such design that was both of these things was the 1995 Sport Spider.

Looking more like a concept car than a production reality, this lightweight (courtesy of its aluminium chassis and composite body panels) sports car was capable of 135mph from its four-cylinder, 16-valve, twin overhead cam 2-litre engine (taken from the Clio Williams), which was situated behind the two-seat compartment.

Early examples had no windscreen, and relied on a deflector to keep the wind and rain from the faces of the driver and passenger: later models conceded this little bit to tradition and came with a screen.

MERCEDES-BENZ F300 LIFE JET

◀ Launched at the 1997 Frankfurt Motor Show, the Life Jet was called a research vehicle and was built to explore the possibilities of bringing the thrills of motorcycling to drivers without exposing them to the dangers associated with the spills. Built from aluminium, the main aeroplane-inspired bodyshell weighed just 89kg, had gullwing doors, and could be converted quickly into a cabriolet by removing two panels from the roof.

As one would expect with a car that was never going to face the realities of production, a number of clever gadgets found their way into it, including headlights controlled by the Active Tilt computer that allowed them to follow the road better. It also came with air-conditioning, and special tyres were developed to cope with the unusually high cornering forces developed by the tilting of the body and suspension.

HYUNDAI NEOS

▼ Almost everyone loves to see innovative thinking, especially from a company that has hitherto produced dull cars with little to dream about. Dull cars may sell, but dream cars and sexy concepts convince the buying public your company has a future.

With this in mind, Hyundai launched the Neos (short for New Evolution Open Sportscar) at the 2000 Paris Motor Show. Its influences included the Plymouth Prowler and the Light Car Company's Rocket, and it was obviously aimed at attracting the attention of buyers who would not previously have included Hyundai on their shopping list due to the lack of exciting product. But here was a hot-rod style car, powered by a mid-mounted 2-litre engine that delivered an estimated 250bhp, with a body made from aluminium, thermoplastic composites, and carbon-fibre strengthening.

This was a Hyundai with excitement written right through it: unfortunately the world is still waiting for its like to make it into production.

CORD 812

▲ Anyone seeing a Cord 812 for the first time in 1935 would have been forgiven for thinking how futuristic it looked. It did, and it was, in many ways, years ahead of its time.

Designed by Gordon Buehrig, it had a superbly aerodynamic shape for the time. Furthermore, its body was of unitary construction, whilst almost all of its rivals were still building cars with separate chassis and bodywork. Its 4.8-litre 115bhp supercharged engine was silky smooth, giving a top speed of 90mph, and although it faced north-south as did all engines at that time, it drove the front wheels, via a semi-automatic gearbox. The interior was equally modern, with a turned chromed dash and superb detailing, including a little handle on each side to wind up the pop-up headlights. With such a pantheon of futuristic delights one might have expected it to be a runaway success, but it was not to be: as other manufacturers have found since, buyers like to be introduced gently to new ideas. This was so far in advance of customer expectations that most would-be buyers were scared off, and it was a sales disaster, being pulled after just two years on sale.

FORD GALAXIE SKYLINER RETRACTABLE

▼ Designing and building cars in the US in the 1950s could rightly be compared to an arms race, with each manufacturer busily trying to out-chrome and glitz their rivals with ever larger, more extravagant designs. Whilst part of the Ford Motor Company was busy committing hara-kiri with the disastrous Edsel, other clearer-thinking elements of the company were engaged on raising not just the competition bar for their rivals, but the roofs off their cars.

We are now familiar with lifting hard-tops, thanks to the Mercedes-Benz SLK *et al*, but in 1957 the idea of pressing a button and watching the huge roof lift up, fold, and then disappear into the trunk was just fantastic, even if it did mean there was little luggage space left with the roof down. But then, who wants to carry luggage when you're out cruisin'?

Blessed with such a party trick, performance didn't matter, but for the record it was capable of 110mph from its 4.5-litre V8. To its owners, however, it was capable of something considerably cooler …

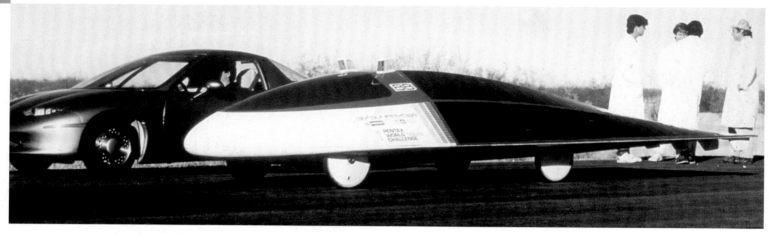

GM SUNRAYCER

▲ It was immediately obvious when looking at the Sunraycer's deliberately misspelt name that this was a car that had a purpose beyond amusing the boffins working in R&D: the marketing boys had shown interest, and a large sum of money had been thrown at the car.

It was built in 1987 to enter a 1,950-mile race across some of the hottest territory in Australia, and some of the other entrants must have felt like packing up and going home when it first arrived. Clad in a staggering 7,200 solar cells, the nearly 20ft long car was powered by a single DC motor driving one of the rear wheels, which also acted as a generator under braking. No one was surprised when the Sunraycer won by a huge margin, but many of us are eagerly awaiting the day when a more practical version becomes available as everyday transport. Cynics would advise such people not to hold their breath whilst waiting.

RENAULT INITIALE

▼ The Renault Initiale of 1995 was one of the world's most luxurious and desirable concept cars, featuring a de-tuned (but at 329bhp, still highly respectable) version of its V10 Formula 1 engine, powering all four wheels and giving a claimed top speed of 190mph.

With designer luggage specially tailored to the car by Louis Vuitton, its interior featured diffused lighting, seats clad in Scottish Bridge of Weir leather, full climate control, video, superb hi-fi, telephone, and a fully glazed roof which stretched from the base of the windscreen to the V-shaped rear screen that formed part of the tail-gate.

Its sharp styling was similar to that of the Lincoln Sentinel from the front, although it seemed more happily concluded at the rear, and it eventually saw the light of day – in heavily watered-down fashion – in the Vel Satis.

RENAULT ÉTOILE FILANTE

▼ The years following the end of the Second World War were strange. For one thing, there were many scientists around Europe and America who had hitherto been employed building fiendish machines aimed at defeating the enemy. Secondly, there was a race on to try and rebuild the economies of many countries, and motor manufacture was seen as playing a crucial role.

It should come as no surprise, therefore, that a number of unusual machines were built in this period, and one such was the Étoile Filante ('shooting star') from Renault. Powered by a 270bhp Turbomeca gas turbine engine that drove the rear wheels, its purpose was experimental as regards its engine, and record-breaking for PR ends. In 1956 it recorded a top speed of 192.5mph on the salt flats at Utah, a class record which stands to this day.

Renault was not alone at this time in experimenting with gas turbine engines, and neither was it alone in deciding ultimately that they offered no real future to mass private transportation.

FORD COCKPIT

▲ Ford's projected view of motoring for the late 1980s and beyond must have been a bleak one judging from their 1981 concept, the Cockpit. Designed during the period of uncertainty following the Iranian Revolution when oil supplies seemed threatened, this three-wheeled two-seater was aimed at providing fun for its occupants, who sat in tandem, whilst costing as little as possible to run, returning a highly respectable 75mpg in city driving. This was achieved by the clever use of a 200cc motorcycle engine actually mounted inside the single rear wheel, and by making the bodywork of lightweight materials throughout. Whilst it is fortunate that such parsimony proved unnecessary, it is a shame that the idea went no further.

CHAPTER FIVE

WHAT A STUNNER!

RINSPEED YELLO TALBO

▶ The Swiss design house of Rinspeed has been responsible for many thought-provoking designs, including the Splash, a car that was also a hydrofoil boat, and the Presto, a car that at the touch of a button could stretch from a two-seater into a full four-seater. For a company of such innovative thinking, the 1996 Yello Talbo (named after the urban/electric rock group Yello) seems positively tame and restrained, but it is nevertheless a terrifically beautiful machine.

Drawing heavily on the shape of a 1938 Talbot Lago 150SS design by Figoni and Falaschi, the car paid due homage to the unquestioned art of the original, including a deliciously trimmed interior in silk, but added plenty of late 1990s technology to make it all the more remarkable. It boasted a supercharged 5-litre V8 engine mated to an automatic gearbox, which produced a 0–60mph sprint time of just 5.5 seconds, courtesy of some 320bhp available on tap.

PORSCHE 911 2.7 RS

▼ Only a true Porsche rivet-counter could tell how many different manifestations of the 911 have been built since its launch in 1964. Virtually all have their fans, and picking out the definitive 911 would normally be very difficult to do, were it not for the existence of the 911 2.7 RS from 1973.

Built as a stripped-out racer (no sound-deadening, and even using thinner glass than in a standard car, to reduce weight) that was also happy in city streets, this lightweight model won praise not only among Porsche fans but also among professional racing drivers such as John Watson and James Hunt. Its flat-six 2.7-litre engine gave 210bhp, and a top speed of 152mph after dismissing the first 60mph in 5.8 seconds. For 1973, these were highly respectable figures, winning it much admiration, which is still reflected today in the price a collector might pay whenever one of the 1,579 examples built comes up for sale.

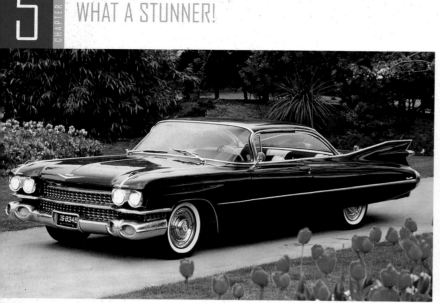

1959 CADILLAC ELDORADAO

▲ Possibly the most arresting car design of all time, the 1959 Cadillac range marked the pinnacle of the 'chrome and fins' era. Its arrival was a truly monumental occasion, and to this day it is hard to imagine a more extravagant machine ever reaching the mass-market that Cadillac were aiming at.

Equipment included auto-transmission, electric windows, power seat adjustment, power hood, air-conditioning, cruise-control, auto-dipping headlights, power quarter-light vents, auto heating, and even a signal-seeking pre-selector radio. Add to this inventory of luxuries the most self-confident of styling ever to leave Detroit, complete with the largest ever fins, topped by twin rocket-ship tail-lamps, and the resulting car could not be anything other than truly striking. Indeed, for many there has never been a finer expression of automotive art than the 1959 Cadillac.

BMW M6

▼ If ruining the day of any Porsche 911 owner is your idea of fun, but you can't quite bring yourself to buying the four-door saloon BMW M5, then 2004's M6 coupé from the same company may hold the solution.

Although powered by the same 500bhp 5-litre V10 found in the saloon, the car is considerably lighter thanks to the extensive use of carbon-fibre panels and aluminium throughout, resulting in a higher bhp/ton ratio and a 0–60mph sprint time of 4.6 seconds, with a governed top speed of 155mph.

This is one huge bruiser of a car, for people who want true, top-flight sports car performance without losing the luxury of a more grown-up car: in short, a 21st-century master car.

MORGAN AEROMAX

▲ The Worcestershire firm of Morgan have built a reputation around hand-crafted sports cars with modern performance but an old-fashioned appearance, and the use of traditional materials such as ash frames for the bodywork. The bug-eyed Aero 8 was the first car to differ from this recipe, but was not to everyone's taste.

The Aeromax, however, launched at the 2005 Geneva Motor Show, is a startling car which somehow manages to blend much of the traditional styling cues with a strikingly modern look. Officially designed as a one-off styling exercise with a customer ready to buy the finished vehicle, this is a terrific car, powered by a BMW-sourced V8 that ensures a thoroughly modern performance, and boasting air-conditioning, air pressure and temperature sensors, airbags, ABS, cruise control, and a set of bespoke luggage designed by Schedoni of Italy.

FAB 1

▶ Devotees of the Gerry Anderson string-fest that was the *Thunderbirds* TV puppet series from the 1960s will forever associate Lady Penelope Creighton-Ward and her chauffeur Parker with the huge six-wheeled Rolls-Royce; but for the 2004 feature film, a new car was built bearing the famous registration FAB 1.

As Parker would have said, 'One has to move with the times, m'lady', and certainly the 21st-century FAB 1 is bang up-to-the-minute. The huge six-wheeler is 23ft long, and its glittering pink coachwork is made from carbon-fibre and Kevlar composite materials, which keeps the weight down to just 1 tonne. With an estimated top speed in excess of 250mph, it can travel on land, water, and air.

Built by the Ford Motor Company, there are currently no plans to put it into production.

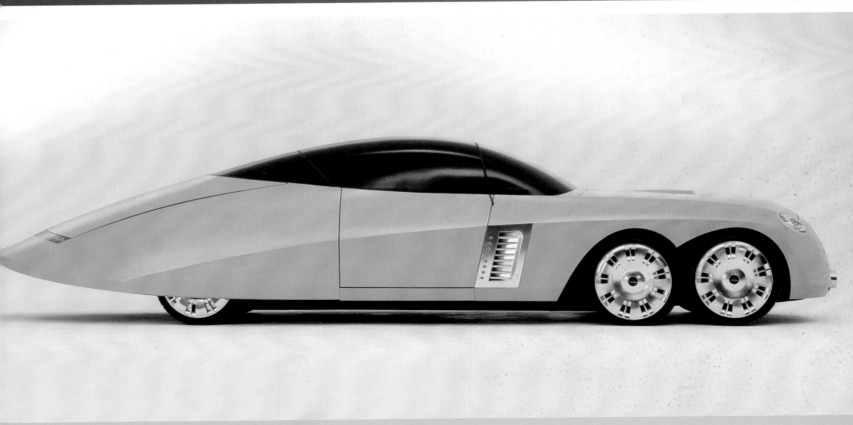

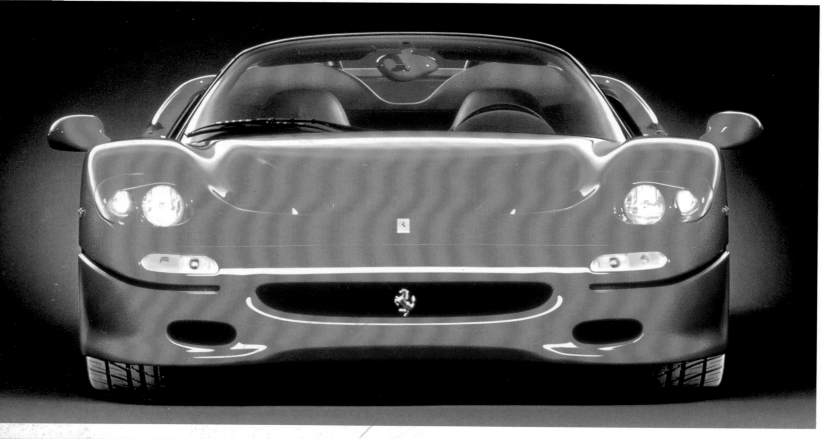

FERRARI F50 BARCHETTA

▲ In recent years, the ever-growing budgets of the Formula 1 teams have created cars which bear less and less relation to even the most extreme of sports cars, and this in turn has led the sport's detractors to question what the point of the whole spectacle is.

The Ferrari F50, however, was the one car in modern times to have rubbished this argument. Whilst the McLaren F1 used elements of F1 technology, such as a carbon-fibre body, the Ferrari F50 was designed as a road-going F1 car, sharing much technology and design language with the car that almost took Alain Prost to another World Championship in 1990. Its 4.7-litre V12 engine was, unlike that of any road-car but exactly like an F1 car, bolted rigidly to the carbon fibre monocoque. Its top speed of 202mph, with a 0–60mph sprint dispatched in 3.7 seconds, was near F1 performance also, but its killer punch had to be its staggering beauty. From any angle, it is pure art, and speaks to the very soul of anyone who is in any way moved by cars and the emotions they stir.

PROJECT KAHN BLACK LABEL DISCOVERY

◀ Off-roaders, and for that matter Land Rovers in particular, have come a long way in the last 30 years. No longer just a farmer's tool, or even just something to tow Dobbin from one gymkhana to the next, they are now probably bought by more city-dwellers and townies than people who really need their considerable off-roading ability.

With that being the case, and bearing in mind what a fashion statement the right set of wheels can make, one should not be unduly surprised to see that the bespoke customisation of the new Land Rover Discovery started so soon after its launch. 2005's Project Kahn Black Label Discovery is a handsome beast equipped with Playstations, DVDs, privacy glass, and high quality leather, as well as 22in wheels to cruise the black-top, if not to crush too much green-stuff.

Performance up-rates are also available on demand to tailor the car's athleticism to the owner's demands, adding further to the bespoke nature of this sharp-suited new kid on the block.

LAMBORGHINI MIURA

▶ The supercar from an Italian tractor manufacturer was one way of describing the Miura when it was launched in 1966, but for many in the UK the first time they saw one was in the opening scenes of the 1969 film *The Italian Job*, accompanied by Matt Monroe crooning his way through *On Days Like These*.

The Miura was a devastatingly beautiful car aimed at stealing business from Ferrari, and was a totally unique piece of design that featured a mid-mounted transverse V12 engine whose noise had to be heard to be believed. Inside, its perfect design was complemented by a fabulously crafted cockpit that bore all the hallmarks of the world-class fashion design with which Italy is associated.

INSPIRATION

◀ Ask any industrial archaeologist which country led the way in steam power, and they'll tell you Great Britain. It should come as no great surprise, therefore – even though steam has long since been replaced as the power behind the country's factories and railway engines – to find British engineers plotting once more to conquer the world with steam.

Working away in Hampshire, a group of enthusiasts, scientists, and technicians have built a machine of rare beauty, whose lines seem far removed from the grimy locomotives one normally associates with steam power. Named Inspiration, this sleek machine is set to break the World Land Speed record for steam vehicles set at 121.57mph back in 1906 by Fred Marriott in a Stanley steamer.

Inspiration's power comes from a steam turbine, and its top speed is calculated to be well in excess of 200mph, with its steam coming from a state-of-the-art LPG-fuelled generator. Whilst its success is unlikely to fuel a wholesale return to steam-powered cars (once thought every bit as viable as petrol), it should open minds to the possibilities modern steam technology can offer.

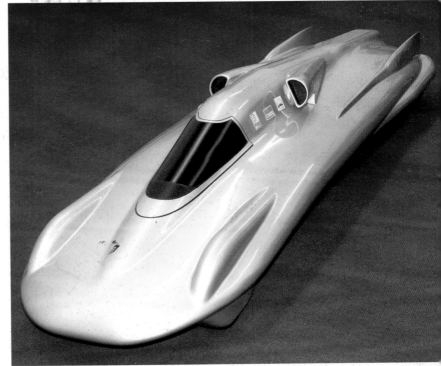

ROVER SD1

▼ For much of its lifetime the Rover Car Company had built slightly staid cars aimed at the middle-classes, and government officials felt quite at home using them as ministerial transport. The long hot summer of 1976, however, saw the launch of a very different kind of Rover, designed by David Bache.

The SD1 was low, very sleek, the only hatchback in its class, and very modern indeed, both inside and out. Originally only available with the Buick-sourced 3.5-litre V8, power and refinement was not a problem, and with the later addition of the Van den Plas model it was capable of competing in the luxury category with the best in its class. Or at least, it should have been. Unfortunately, poor quality steel led to premature rusting, and build quality – as with most of the BL range at this time – was best described as patchy.

Thus fell from grace a car that deserved much better, and had the looks to achieve what only shoddy workmanship and inferior materials held back.

MENTLEY INSANNE

▲ The Mentley Insanne is the work of world-renowned car customiser Andy Saunders of Poole, England. Starting with a crash-damaged Bentley Mulsanne Turbo, he removed the roof and, creating new pillars front and rear, fabricated a new half-glazed roof panel which now sits 3in lower than on a standard Bentley. The front and rear lights are from a Range Rover, as are the side louvres. With lowered suspension, a set of dazzling 20in chrome alloy wheels give the car a real presence, whilst its Bentley grille is also lowered and stretched to complement the car's new proportions.

Whilst there are those who feel that customising a Bentley is almost sacrilegious, it is hard to fault Saunders's work, which has brought him high acclaim, and the Mentley Insanne has won much praise and several prestigious awards since it first appeared in 2003.

SALEEN S7

▶ Steve Saleen started out racing Ford Mustangs in the Trans-Am series, and from there went into selling modified Mustangs. His first car of his own design, however, the S7, has been called America's only true supercar, and whether or not this is being unkind to other US fast car manufacturers, it is undeniably worthy of membership to the exclusive elite of cars extreme enough to be called supercars.

Launched in 2001, it is powered by a 7-litre 550bhp V8 engine that can hurl the car from standstill to 60mph in less than 4 seconds and can comfortably break the 200mph barrier flat out. It is claimed that the extreme ground effects employed which guarantee its stability could, theoretically, hold the car to an upside down road at 160mph, although this has not been put to the test. What is beyond dispute is its fantastic appearance and true supercar qualities, with its sumptuous cabin complementing perfectly its dramatic exterior.

ROLLS-ROYCE SILVER GHOST

◄ The Rolls-Royce Silver Ghost was a car whose magnificence it is hard to exaggerate. Launched in 1907, just three years after C.S. Rolls had joined forces with engineer Henry Royce, it was a technical *tour de force*, whose excellence and reliability was put to the test in a number of startling ways, including driving from London to Edinburgh (on roads much poorer and less direct than those we enjoy today) in top gear throughout.

   Powered by a 7-litre, straight six engine, which is itself something of a work of art, the lines of early examples – such as this from 1909, on show at the National Motor Museum, Beaulieu – are so perfectly executed and give it such a majestic presence that it is easy to see how fully it deserves the title 'The finest motor-car in the world'.

ISDERA COMMENDATORE 112I

▲ The lesson that the McLaren F1 taught the Jaguar XJ220 was a simple one: big cars are not necessarily the fastest. The designers at Isdera, however, appear not to have been listening at that particular moment, as their supercar, the made-to-order Commendatore of 1993, was huge. Its ultra-sleek bodywork was hand-built, and featured not only gullwing doors and an external rear-view mirror but also matching gullwing covers which opened to display the 408bhp Mercedes-Benz sourced 6-litre V12 engine.

   With much of the remaining running gear coming from Porsche, its top speed of 214mph and 0–60 sprint time of just 4.7 seconds should come as no surprise.

HISPANO SUIZA H6C

◀ For one glorious decade, starting at the end of the First World War and ending with the Wall Street Crash, the words 'luxury car' did not necessarily mean Rolls-Royce or Mercedes-Benz. Names such as Pierce-Arrow, Duesenberg, Bugatti, Packard, and Hispano-Suiza were all competing for the attentions of the super-rich with ever more glamorous designs, and although many limped on after the crash, the depression that followed meant the customers were no longer there in the same numbers, and slowly these companies failed.

One car of exotic proportions and striking appearance was the Hispano Suiza H6C. Powered by an 8-litre in-line six with overhead cam, it was good for 85mph, and a number of bodies were put on the chassis of the 264 examples built, including this thoroughly splendid example from 1924, made from tulip-wood, with all the skill and craftsmanship of the top boat-builders of the time. Once raced by the wealthy tycoon Andre Dubonnet, it still exists, in glorious condition.

TVR SAGARIS

▼ The Blackpool-based firm TVR have produced many wild and exciting cars in their history, but few can rival the 2004 Sagaris for sheer presence, whilst not forgetting the principles behind all TVRs: speed and fun by the bucket-load.

There can be few cars ever to have been launched with so much of their bodywork already cut away, but on the Sagaris the huge vents liberally sprinkled across its surfaces still manage to complement its basic svelte shape. Performance is a given, and does not fail to please: 0–60mph in 3.6 seconds (or put another way, 0.9 seconds faster than a Ferrari 360 Modena), and a top speed of 194mph from its 32-valve, 400bhp, 4-litre, six-cylinder power-plant. Whilst £50,000 should never be called 'cheap', in relative terms, the Sagaris certainly delivers plenty of bangs per buck.

DODGE CUSTOM ROYAL

▲ Some cars just wouldn't look right without white-wall tyres, and this is most certainly true of the chrome-bedecked cruisers rolling off the production lines of Detroit in the late 1950s.

One such car was the extravagantly styled 1959 Dodge Custom Royal, whose size and stature were greatly exaggerated by the complex and elegantly sculpted chrome grille, its chromed eyebrows, two-tone paintwork, and fins which started at the forward end of the rear doors and grew as they went back. Performance was provided courtesy of a big V8 engine, whose 6,276cc gave out an impressive 345bhp, much of which was no doubt needed to haul the car's oversized bulk to its highly respectable top speed of 110mph.

Luxuriously equipped in every way imaginable, one wag noted at the time that there was 'power assistance for everything except the ashtray'.

OVERFINCH RANGE ROVER 580S

▼ The Range Rover has come a very long way since its launch in 1970, and for many years it has attracted the attentions of high performance tuning firms, personalising the ultimate 4x4.

Foremost among such companies are Overfinch, who have consistently sought to improve the Range Rover with both handling kits and performance boost, as well as personalising the exterior and interior appearance of the Solihull classic.

The 580S is the latest (2005) embodiment of the company's philosophy, and features a supercharged 4.2-litre V8 engine which delivers a minimum of 500bhp and a 0–60 sprint time of less than 6 seconds. Complete with its subtle body alteration and interior upgrades, Overfinch believe that this is the 'ultimate all-purpose, all-season supercar'.

FORD RS200

▲ The Ford Motor Company were spectacularly unsuccessful in their timings when they decided to re-enter rallying in the mid-1980s. Prior to the arrival of the Audi Quattro their Escorts had reigned supreme, so Ford spent many millions developing the RS200, aimed squarely at regaining their past glories. In order to homologate the car 200 examples had to be built, and this was undertaken by Reliant of Tamworth, more noted for their three-wheelers than rally beasts.

In rally trim, the 1,800cc mid-mounted four-cylinder engine could deliver 380bhp through all four wheels, and the car was a Group B rally contender from its first outing. It was launched in 1986, a year in which there were, unfortunately, a number of fatalities in rallying that resulted in the banning, after just one season for the RS200, of Group B rally cars, which were judged to be just too fast. After the end of the season, Ford decided to sell the rest of the production run as Ghia-specced road cars: fast, furious, exceptionally rare, and hugely desirable.

JAGUAR E TYPE SERIES 1

◄ When thinking of the Swinging Sixties, the Jaguar E Type was as much a part of the scene as the Mini, the miniskirt, and the Beatles.

Launched in 1961 to replace the XK150, its sublime shape was the work of Malcolm Sayer, who had previously worked on the racing C and D Types. Very few cars look just as good in either roadster or coupé style, but the E Type most definitely did, and it went as well as it looked, although the 150mph top speed boasted of at launch demanded some tinkering and a cruel driver to achieve from the early examples.

What won it over 15,000 sales in a four-year period, however, was that it had the racing pedigree and heritage descended from Le Mans winners, and it offered Ferrari looks and performance for a third of the price of the Italian thoroughbred.

ROLLS-ROYCE 100EX

▼ The 100EX was a concept car based on the huge Phantom, and was launched at the 2004 Geneva Motor Show as a part of the company's centenary celebrations.

Built around an aluminium space-frame, this glorious open-tourer was a full four-seater, with the rear-hinged 'suicide-doors' carried over from its big sister. Hints of the golden era of coachbuilding were all over the car, such as the dramatic use of bleached teak in various locations, polished aluminium trim, and Dark Curzon leather upholstery.

Designed at BMW's Designworks studios in Southern California, so good has the response been that there are rumours of possible limited production, giving Rolls-Royce a replacement for the much-loved Corniche model which died when BMW took over stewardship of the company in 1998.

TATRA 77

▲ The Hans Ledwinka designed Tatra 77 caused a huge stir when launched in 1934 to a stunned motoring world. Here was a fantastically streamlined masterpiece, which showed how slippery designs can be pleasant and need not look like the awkward Chrysler Airflow.

Its styling, however, was just one of its unorthodox features. It featured a 3-litre 90-degree V8 that was placed behind the rear wheels, and was air-cooled. Capable of 85mph, it was a brave driver who explored the outer limits of its performance, as its handling – courtesy of the heavy engine so far back and tricky swing axle rear suspension – was best described as somewhat wayward and unwieldy.

JAGUAR PIRANA

◀ The Pirana of 1967 was a stunning design based on the chassis and running gear of a Series 2 Jaguar E Type, and was designed by Nuccio Bertone of Turin for the *Daily Telegraph*, sponsors of the London Motor Show.

Its luxurious interior was everything one would expect of an up-market Gran Tourer, with plenty of Connolly hide in evidence, air conditioning, electric windows, etc. It was a real runner rather than merely a show car, powered by Jaguar's much-loved 4.2-litre engine.

If its shape seems strangely familiar, that is because whilst only the one Pirana was built and went no further badged as a Jaguar, the shape survived and with little modification went on to become an Italian supercar in 1970, when it re-emerged as the Lamborghini Espada.

THE MONKEEMOBILE

▼ A crucial part of the hit TV series *The Monkees* was the Monkeemobile, created by Custom Car designer Dean Jeffries in just three weeks in 1967. General Motors provided him with two new Pontiac GTO convertibles for the project and he set to work.

The end result was a 21ft long ultra-cool semi-dragster, whose highly tuned and modified 389cu in GTO V8 protruded proudly out of the bonnet and was neatly topped off with a GMC supercharger. Painted in candy apple red, its interior was trimmed in white Naugahyde and had four bucket seats, with a rear bench seat for the band's instruments. Happily, while the band have long since gone their separate ways (apart from occasional reunions) this example of sixties cool still exists.

RUSS MEEKS' 1923 T ROADSTER

▲ Obviously not a street-legal machine, Russ Meeks' 1923 T Roadster is a car that has been undergoing constant modification for the past 36 years, and has been on many occasions to El Mirage and the Bonneville Salt Flats to compete in race week.

Its body is made from hand-formed and polished aluminium panels attached to a chrome-molybdenum tube chassis, and it is powered by a 1952 GMC 322cu in engine that is injected with its Nitrous-Oxide fuel, in the best traditions of super-fast dragster machines.

An undeniably striking machine, it illustrates the level of art achievable in the custom cars of today, and looks decidedly rapid even when standing still.

AUDI AVUS QUATTRO

▼ The Ingolstadt-based firm of Audi have long held a reputation as innovative thinkers, but when in 1991 they unveiled the Avus Quattro the motoring world stopped in its tracks and looked on in amazement.

Here was an aluminium-bodied two-seater with a purity of form that was simply breathtaking. It featured a unique W12 engine of 6 litres that developed 509bhp, which allowed the four-wheel-drive machine to blast up to its top speed of 210mph, cracking the first 60mph from standstill in a barely believable 3 seconds. Entry was via scissor doors, and once inside the minimalist approach which left the exterior unadorned with anything unnecessary continued, the designers, eschewing the desire for cockpit-style gauges and switch-gear which seek only to flatter, keeping everything uncluttered and purposeful.

6

WHAT THE . . ?

ITALA

▶ It might look like just another crude veteran car, but the Itala racer from 1907 was a supercar of its day, and even today it is worthy of huge respect.

Its 14.9-litre four-cylinder engine looks more suited to powering an ocean liner than a car, and was capable of propelling the Itala and its two occupants to speeds of up to 100mph. This may not sound too fast, but it should be borne in mind that the front wheels (whose wooden spokes don't look up to the job of steering such a heavy machine, with its high centre of gravity, around bends at high speed) had no brakes attached to them, and these cars raced predominantly on unmade Continental roads which were not closed to other road-users. It is hard to imagine just how frightening such a machine must have been at full tilt, but with the almost total lack of meaningful control they make today's F1 cars seem remarkably tame.

The idea of road safety is a concept which, it would appear, grew up as a result of experience, much of it gained the hard and costly way with machines such as the Itala racer.

McLEAN V8 MONOWHEEL

▼ The monowheel is not a new invention by any stretch of the imagination, but fitting a V8 into one, and then somehow managing to license it for use on public roads, most definitely is.

That is the unique claim to fame of 47-year-old Kerry McLean of Walled Lake, Michigan, USA. His monowheel uses a water-cooled Buick engine, and McLean has to date recorded a top speed of 53mph on the Bonneville Salt Flats, but aims to break the 100mph barrier in due course.

Stability at speed can be a major cause for concern with monowheels, and the brave, or perhaps foolhardy, McLean will need to address this issue if he is to achieve three figures on his machine rather than the three letters R, I, and P.

BROOKE SWAN

▲ One of the most bizarre cars ever built must surely be the Brooke-based Swan, made for an Englishman living in Calcutta in 1909.

Brooke had started out in Suffolk as millwrights, boiler-makers, and brass and iron founders, turning their hands to making cars in 1901. The Swan was most definitely a one-off eccentricity, built to order by R.N. Mathewson. The chassis and body were made in India, and then shipped to England where the six-cylinder Brooke engine was fitted.

The Swan is more, however, than mere ornament: its eyes can be made to light up, and its beak can open and close, whilst the car's exhaust can be directed through a whistle in the neck, allowing it to hiss. It can even spray a jet of water from the same opening. Happily, this most odd car still exists.

DODGE RAM SRT 10

◄ When pickup trucks were first designed their purpose was purely utilitarian, hence the term 'Ute' in Australia. The art of marketing, however, is all about making your product more attractive than that of your rivals, and so, over a period of time, even pickups have had the glamour stick waved liberally over them. Perhaps the most extreme of trucks currently available, and in the words of its manufacturer 'the world's fastest production pickup truck', is the Dodge Ram SRT 10.

Long since having forgotten its humble origin, the Ram SRT 10 goes all out to obliterate any opposition, with 500bhp coming from its 8.3-litre V10 engine borrowed from the Viper. Sitting proudly on its 22in alloy wheels it looks like a scaled-down truck, but with a $50,00 price-tag its 0–60 sprint time of under 5 seconds and top speed of 154mph are most un-truck like.

NISSAN CHAPEAU

▶ Some of motoring's most bizarre concepts have come from Japan, a country that seems uniquely gifted in being able to look at something commonplace and redesign it thoroughly from a totally new and unexpected perspective.

A good example of this is the Nissan Chapeau of 1989, a monstrous wheeled-box, where the designers started on the inside and worked outwards. It was aimed at a sophisticated future generation of city-dwellers, who – presumably because they'll spend so much time in traffic jams – will apparently look on their cars as more than mere transport. Accordingly, video games, computers, and complex entertainment systems were fitted. Nevertheless, one cannot but feel that if the designers had spent a little less time designing the interior of a home on wheels, the exterior could have ended up looking slightly less like a mobile house and more like a desirable car.

I.D.E.A. KAZ

▼ It is a widely accepted piece of logic, derived from many decades of experiment, that for most passenger vehicles the optimum number of wheels needed to make contact with terra firma is four. However, the designers of the huge limousine from 2001 known as Kaz (Keio Advanced Zero-emission vehicle) believed that twice that amount would be a much better idea.

Furthermore, as well as involving six of the wheels in steering the bizarre machine, each of the eight wheels was powered by its own electric motor. If one accepts that one of the principal functions of a limousine is to attract attention, then it can be said that the Kaz would be highly efficient should it ever make it into production, although a classier name would be a good way of off-setting the ridicule it might draw from its appearance.

WHAT THE ...?

WESTFIELD MEGABUSA

▼ A kit car fitted with a four-cylinder 1,300cc engine doesn't sound like the most exciting recipe for a fun sports car. But when the engine is the DOHC lump from the Suzuki GSXR1300R Hayabusa, and the kit car's name is Westfield, it is wise to put aside any reservations one might have: this is one truly mighty machine.

Sprinting from 0–60mph in 3.48 seconds is no mean achievement, and provided the driver can stop the rear wheels from spinning, with a power-to-weight-ratio of 420bhp per tonne, this is the sort of neck-wrenching performance the pocket-rocket has on offer. Lightweight materials and a space-frame chassis are all part of the potent mix, as is the sequential six-speed gearbox, which makes the car ideal for track-day fun as well as normal road use. A top speed of 138mph may sound rather tame for such a monster, but as with rally cars, acceleration in the Westfield is of greater importance than the double-ton.

If building is not part of the owner's plan, it can be bought ready for the road.

SAINT HORSE ANGEL

▶ The Jinma (Saint Horse) Angel is an amazing car from the People's Republic of China. Known locally as a 'grandfather car', it obviously draws heavily – although not entirely successfully – on 1930s design themes. These modern machines are powered by 2.3-litre engines, and are capable of a top speed of just 75mph. In fairness to the car, however, it should be said that appearance is more important than performance, although the ability to show a clean pair of heels to legal teams keen to sue for infringement of Rolls-Royce trademarks with respect to the car's Parthenon radiator grille and imitation Spirit of Ecstasy mascot might be useful.

It should not come as too great a surprise to learn that the Saint Horse Angel is a favourite as a wedding car in China. No examples are known to have been exported to the West to date.

ARBEL

◀ The 1958 Arbel, from France, was the final development of a car that had started out several years previously, known then as the Symetric. Its bizarre, barrel-shaped body was formed around three hoops that fitted onto a spinal tube that doubled up as the car's fuel tank.

Originally it had used a 1,100cc four-cylinder engine to power four electric motors, one on each wheel, but the Arbel of 1958 offered motive power from either a rotary petrol engine, a Genestat gas-turbine, or, most preposterously of all, a Genestatom nuclear reactor. Had this option ever taken to the roads, one can scarcely imagine how much more dangerous our lives would have become in the event of one being involved in a road accident.

Other luxuries included automatically emptying ashtrays (onto the road), phosphorescent bumpers, telephone, tape recorder, windscreen washer automatically topped up by rain-water, and even an electric razor. The car never sold, and before long disappeared, leaving behind many unpaid debts.

HONDA INSIGHT MAX POWER

▼ When Honda's engineers and scientists set about designing an electric-hybrid vehicle, they knew they were not simply designing a show car which would wow the crowds at a few shows before being wheeled into a storeroom somewhere never to be seen again, or at best end up in a company museum.

No, this was going to be a real car, to be driven by owners, not just by scientists on test routes. It would, therefore, have to be able to perform in real-world scenarios, and there could be no excuses for temperamental idiosyncrasies. The car succeeded in almost every area, returning very pleasing mpg figures of over 80mpg, and although it was never intended as a mass-market machine it found eager buyers who by and large turned into happy owners.

The one area where it under-performed was in its general appearance, which was considerably less inspired than the clever technology that lurked underneath the awkward shape. Step forward *Max Power* magazine, whose readers are devotees of fast cars with high performance and flash paint work: finding an example with 100,000 miles under its wheels, in 1999 they set to work modifying and customising this already unusual car. The result is startling rather than attractive, but shows that worthy, planet-saving machinery does not have to be dull.

RENAULT ESPACE F1

▲ Most people will agree that whilst MPVs are, in general, a highly practical option for families, they are not sexy, or fun, and are bought by people for whom their sporting days are something of a fading memory.

One MPV against which such charges of pedestrian transport cannot be levelled, however, is the 1994 Renault Espace F1. Its 3.5-litre V10 engine, rear axle, and gearbox all came straight from the Formula 1 world championship winning Williams FW14 racing car. Naturally, performance was somewhat beyond the norm for this style of vehicle, and its top speed of almost 190mph would be sufficient to soothe the ego of any ex-boy racer now turned family man. However, this was strictly a one-off built for promotional purposes.

DAIHATSU TREK

▲ The 1990 Trek concept from Japanese manufacturer Daihatsu is a car which offers a possible answer to a question no one had previously thought needed asking. Full marks should be awarded to its inventor for sheer ingenuity, but most motorists prefer to use their cars for transport in either a work or a recreational context, and then retire home or to their caravan, hotel, or lodgings.

What the single-seat Trek offers, however, is the ability to drive out to somewhere really remote, then fold away the seat, steering-column, and roll-over hoop, leaving a flat platform on which to sleep. And for lovers of John Wayne westerns, a few minutes' work can convert the comfy bed platform into a modern interpretation of a Wild West covered wagon. Incoming flaming arrows from angered natives may be less of a danger for the sleeping inhabitant, however, than the sound of uncontrollable laughter from passers-by.

BATMOBILE

▶ When the *Batman* TV series aired in the late 1960s, the car all youngsters believed was the coolest belonged to a part-time caped crusader who lived a double life as millionaire Bruce Wayne. As Batman, his job was to capture villains such as the Penguin and the Riddler, and his home-grown supercar, which played a crucial role in this task, was the Batmobile.

Built on the platform of a Ford concept car, the Lincoln Futura, its styling and gadgets were the handiwork of Hollywood master customiser George Barris. Its fibreglass bodywork was painted in 40 coats of acrylic black velvet-glow bat fuzz, with orange outlines. Gadgets included parachutes, twin aircraft-style perspex bullet-proof windshields, batscope, etc. Power came from a Ford Mustang 428cu in V8 engine, and the car cost $75,000 to build, at a time when that was considered a lot of money.

Happily, the car still exists, although is no longer actively involved in crime-fighting.

PININFARINA PFX

▼ Throughout the history of the car, designers have toyed with many recurring ideas, with varying levels of success. One particular idea that has been revisited at least once in most decades has been the positioning of the four wheels in a diamond formation, with the front and rear wheels doing the steering and the middle pair being responsible for the car's propulsion.

In 1960, aiming to reduce aerodynamic drag, the Italian styling house of Pininfarina decided to look anew at this layout with the PFX. The result was an egg-shaped curiosity, with the still obligatory fins at the rear, nominally for stability but principally for contemporary styling benefit. Developed from a patented design from Alberto Morelli, its wheels were actually in a rhomboid formation, and were powered by a 1,100cc four-cylinder engine.

After extensive testing, no manufacturers were found who showed interest in the concept, and it went no further – principally, it is suspected, because wheels located in this formation invariably lead to extremely sensitive and twitchy handling, which would never be palatable to the motoring public.

9F-V400

▼ 9F-V400 is probably not the most imaginative name ever given to a car: indeed, it sounds more like a Japanese racing motorcycle than the fastest car tested to date at Italy's Nardo test track.

Based on a Porsche 911 GT2, the primary weapon in its successful attack on the McLaren F1's previous record of 240.1mph (set in 1998 and now beaten by just 1mph) is a heavily tuned twin-turbo 3.8-litre flat-six engine that develops 828bhp, with the help of forged titanium con-rods, forged aluminium pistons, reworked KKK turbos, and water-cooled inter-coolers. Bringing the car's weight down to 1,300kg has been achieved by replacing metal panels such as the roof, bonnet, and engine lid with carbon-fibre, resulting in a highly impressive power to weight ratio of 637bhp per tonne.

Such extremes never come cheap, however, and with a price-tag of £278,000 the production numbers of this car, built by German tuning firm 9F, will only ever be minuscule, in stark contrast to the performance figures.

MARLIN SPORTSTER

◄ The Marlin Sportster may look like something a cloth-cap-wearing grandad might buy in which to reminisce about the good old days as he clogs up the roads on a sunny Sunday afternoon, but, depending on what engine is installed, this is one car that most definitely has 21st-century power available.

Supplied as a kit of parts from its manufacturer in Crediton, Devon (a place more normally associated with cream teas and ice-cream than insanely fast cars), most of them use engines and mechanicals from a BMW saloon that has probably had its life curtailed by inept driving and an unplanned meeting with a hedge, bus stop, brick wall or other similarly unforgiving obstacle. That might be an engine from a standard 320, or it could just as easily be from an M5: the choice is entirely up to the bravery or sanity of the person assembling his kit. 0–60mph in less than 4 seconds is therefore eminently achievable, whilst for the criminally insane a Chevrolet 5.7-litre V8 is an equally feasible proposition.

It has all the looks of a pre-war sports car, with the performance potential of a modern very hot hatch. Stand aside, grandad, this one's not for you.

ASTON MARTIN DB5 SHOOTING BRAKE

▶ Rumour has it that David Brown (whose initials precede the number in most Aston Martin model names) was a firm fan of the DB5 when it originally came out, but found life a little too cosy with himself, dogs, and other clutter in the car. There was also the added irritation of his canine chums appreciating the car's leather upholstery in a uniquely expensive way, so he had the factory turn his own car into a one-off Shooting Brake (an Estate, in modern parlance).

The end result was actually surprisingly handsome, although the car lost some of its structural rigidity in the conversion, and it was not long before other Aston owners were seeking similar conversions to their own vehicles. Due to the factory's workload being happily too great, the work was handed over to Harold Radford, who built a further 12 examples.

Performance figures were as with the standard DB5, but the cost of conversion made this a particularly expensive way of transporting dogs in the 1960s.

CHRYSLER 300C

◀ Belonging very much to the 'my fins are bigger than yours' era of 1950s' American car styling, the Chrysler 300C was fast, if not attractive to look at. Its huge chrome grille added another element of aggression to a car that already looked mean.

Launched in 1954, the '300' in its title referred to the brake horsepower output from its 331cu in V8 engine that was so devastating at that time in NASCAR, and by 1957 this had risen to 392cu in and 375bhp. Make no mistake, this was a fearsomely rapid machine, although its handling on anything other than straight roads demanded nerves of steel. Its top speed of 135mph was therefore a figure that for the more sensible owner remained a proud boast of potential rather than experience.

VOLVO 850 BTCC RACER

▼ For many decades, Volvo had steadily and deliberately built up a reputation for solid, reliable, durable, and safe, if slightly dull, cars, and had enjoyed healthy sales as a result. At the beginning of the 1990s, however, they decided they needed to appeal more to the heart than the cautious head of an elderly accountant, and so went racing.

Their new car, the 850, seemed the best bet, so they approached TWR to achieve their goals. 1994 saw Volvo appear in the BTCC events, and they decided – laughing at their tweedy Estate car image – to enter two 290bhp 850 Estates for the first season, and on one occasion even placed a cardboard cut-out of a Labrador in the back. For the 1995 season they switched to saloon bodies, which they continued to use until 1997, when they switched to the more compact S40. The Swedish cars achieved more success than many had predicted, and in so doing were able to improve the company's image generally and appeal to a younger clientele.

GEMBALLA GT 750 AERO 3

◄ Porsche's Cayenne will never win any awards for good looks, and many might argue that this was one car the Stuttgart company should not have built. Most, however, will be saying that without having come across 2005's Gemballa customised version of the ugly machine, which in GT 750 trim is capable of a mind-boggling 196mph. From a 4x4! The 750 in its name refers to the bhp output.

The contentious bodywork has been submitted to some serious fettling as well as the mechanical bits: 22in wheels with low-profile tyres more suited to high speed than deep mud replace the standard Porsche items, whilst the inside has likewise received the attentions of the in-house designers to create that special, bespoke atmosphere so necessary in a car such as this.

No longer a serious mud-plugger, and too unwieldy to be a true sports car in spite of its near 200mph performance, this ultra-poseur seems to be a car without purpose and as such, could be argued to be a uniquely compromised machine.

MINI XXL

◀ When BMW Group eventually rolled out the replacement for the 1959 Alec Issigonis original Mini most people agreed immediately that it was better in almost every way than its predecessor, but it was widely noted that the new car had grown somewhat, and some felt it had lost some of its cheeky cuteness.

Those who missed the petiteness of the original may now feel, however, that they were barking up the wrong tree, following the appearance at the 2004 Athens Olympics of the MINI XXL. It started out as a MINI Works Cooper S with John Cooper Works tuning kit, before arriving in Los Angeles for some 'surgery'. The end result was a six-wheeled, six-seat extreme MINI, complete with retractable flat-screen TV, DVD, air-conditioning, and full-length sunroof. At the rear of the car, however, lurked the most surprising add-on: a whirlpool big enough for two people, hidden under the removable roof-panel.

Only two examples have been built.

BAIYUN JMC BOATCAR

▶ Throughout the history of the car there have been a number of designers who have sought a more demanding challenge than merely designing a more competent car than anyone else's. For them, a car should do more than go well on, and in some cases off, the road, and some have designed flying cars, hovercars, and even amphibious cars.

The Baiyun JMC Boatcar of 2003 from the People's Republic of China is one such amphibian. Available in either left- or right-hand drive, the Boatcar has a body (or should that be hull?) made from stainless steel, which is fixed to the chassis of an Isuzu 4x4 Pickup, powered by a diesel engine. Options include air-conditioning, CD, electric windows, and a very useful GPS system.

Most amphibious cars are heavily compromised both on and off road, and the Boatcar is no exception: apart from its bizarre appearance, a top speed on land of just 68mph, and a water-bound top speed of just 7.5mph, says all one needs to know.

SALINE WARRIOR

▲ Lovers of the unassuming and docile Reliant Rialto may see the Saline Warrior in a different way to most other people. Designed and built in just two days (although the paintwork was finished later), this piece of automotive eccentricity was the result of BBC TV programme *Panic Mechanics*, recorded in 2000, in which two teams competed against each other to build a car, and at the end of the two days had to race them.

The Saline Warrior, masterminded by Andy Saunders, won the contest, achieving a top speed of more than 85mph from its original Reliant engine, slightly helped by the addition of a turbocharger. Apart from this mechanical fiddling, it had its roof lowered by 6in, a roll cage built into it, bucket seats fitted, and its bonnet stretched by 20in to give it the appearance of a Bonneville Salt Flats racer. After the competition Saunders finished the car, and it is now completely street legal, albeit something of a distraction for other motorists.

WHAT THE ...?

ISUZU NAGISA

▼ Every so often a car comes along that looks so inherently daft that one is left almost speechless. One such car was the Isuzu Nagisa, a concept car that aimed to join the short list of cars one could intentionally drive into water.

With the 1991 Nagisa form definitely followed function, and it should come as no surprise that it floated, as it looked very much like a cabin-cruiser. The problem with cars that try to accommodate two functions is that very rarely are they able to perform either to any great degree of competence, and as the rules that dictate what makes a good boat vary so much from those relating to car design, any vehicle – Nagisa included – that tries to do both will be a huge compromise of both sets of principles, resulting in both a deeply flawed boat and a deeply flawed car.

The fact that the Nagisa sank out of view after the 1991 motor shows bears testimony to its inability to sail or drive with any degree of panache.

CURTISS-WRIGHT AIRCAR

▲ Cars are great on tarmac, and some do fairly well off-road also, but they need different tyres, long-travel suspension, and are not to everyone's taste, especially the off-road cars of the late 1950s. Step forward the 1959 Curtiss-Wright Aircar.

The Aircar, and hoped-for subsequent Bee (illustrated), were hovercars that belonged more in science fiction than science fact. The idea was simple, but executing it led to tears, headaches (from the tremendous noise levels from the two examples built), and ultimately bankruptcy for the Curtiss-Wright company that built them. The final irony was that with no flexible skirt, and a hover height of just inches above ground level, they were completely useless on anything other than the smoothest of tarmac and proved nearly impossible to control. The US Military had a look at the working prototypes, which clocked up just 25 hours flight time between them, but soon arrived at the obvious conclusion: nice try, but no cigar.

LIGHTBURN ZETA

▶ Those who believe that the only Australian motor manufacturer is Holden are doing the continent a huge injustice, as there have been over 100 attempts to found car firms there.

One company launched with misplaced high hopes was Lightburn, who had previous experience of making machinery such as concrete mixers and power-tools. Their contribution to motoring madness came in 1963 with the launch of the bizarre-looking Zeta, whose front wheels were powered by a 328cc Villiers engine. One unexpected design feature that delighted owners was the ability to remove the seats and fix them to the roof to provide a grandstand-viewing platform for sporting events.

Hopes of building and selling 50 of these fibreglass carbuncles per week proved highly optimistic, and in the event just 363 sold from 1963–66.

PEUGEOT VROOMSTER

◀ As its name suggests, the Vroomster concept of 2000 was neither fully thought-out nor particularly sensible. In fact, the less kind may suggest it would be a front-runner in the daftest car contest.

Features like the elongated windscreen, the handlebar steering, and the fuel tank being placed between the legs of the driver, are things that one feels may not make it to production reality. The bodywork, meanwhile, is made from carbon-fibre and aims to combine the freedom of a motorcycle and the safety of a car, with performance supplied by a 110bhp twin-cam 16-valve engine.

Such concepts are part of the necessary development process of the car as a species, and whilst often extreme they encourage the car-buying public to accept slightly less extreme advances in design.

URBAN GORILLA LIMOUSINE

▲ The designers of the original Hummer were working to a strict brief: to build a machine suitable for the rigours of the battlefield — and judging by the number of Hummers to be found in the world's various conflict zones, it could be said that by and large they achieved this aim. It is very doubtful if the same designers ever dreamt there would be a day when their brutally minimalist machine would become the car of choice of members of the Hollywood *glitterati*, but that's showbiz.

Neither is it likely that they could have foreseen the embracing of their design by Kit Car manufacturers, but fact is often stranger than fiction, and one such company offering look-alike Hummers is the mysteriously named Urban Gorilla. Among their catalogue of designs, they even offer a stretched limousine for the truly shameless. Built using the vital organs of some of America's biggest SUVs, they are big, heavy, and clumsy, and are unlikely to sell in significant numbers outside of the USA.

7

DRINK PROBLEMS

BLUEBIRD CN7

▶ Donald Campbell's exploits in the Bluebird CN7 were gripping stuff in the early 1960s, including 1964 when he took the World Land Speed Record at 409mph. With the record standing at not far from double that now, this may not seem so startlingly fast, but the Bluebird was the last car but one to be wheel-driven: all recent attempts have been in cars that were essentially free-wheeling chassis powered by either jet or rocket propulsion.

Built on an aluminium honeycomb chassis and clothed in alloy body panels, the Bluebird cost £1 million to construct – a huge sum at the time. Having crashed in 1960, it was rebuilt and had its rear tail added for increased stability, before finally achieving its goal on 17 July 1964, burning its fuel at a rate of just 1.5mpg.

NAPIER-RAILTON

▼ The glory days of Brooklands Racing Circuit, the world's first purpose-built racetrack, are the stuff of legend, and much of the atmosphere can be experienced by a visit to what is left of the site. A principal exhibit in the museum built in the old Clubhouse is the Napier-Railton, a one-off special, which, driven by Land Speed Record breaker John Cobb, holds the all-time lap record at Brooklands.

Powered by a monstrous 22.3-litre, 450bhp, 12-cylinder Napier-Lion aero-engine, its speed potential is obvious, and is visually accentuated by its startlingly brutal and yet captivating appearance. Built in 1933, its top speed was around 165mph. It had just three gears, and brakes on the rear wheels only, and it drank fuel at a rate of just 5mpg. Pit stops could be a lengthy process, as a complete fill-up from empty takes a full 10 minutes.

ZIL 41047

▲ The imaginatively named ZIL 41047 is the huge limousine favoured by the President of Russia when out and about either at home or abroad.

Obviously borrowing various styling cues from luxury car makers around the globe, it is a strange-looking machine with large amounts of chrome embellishing its enormous bodywork, wheel trims that resemble those fitted to 1970s Rolls-Royce Silver Shadows, and an upright radiator grille that mimics those on Rolls-Royces, Cadillacs, and Lincolns among others.

Powered by a huge 7.7-litre V8 that delivers 315bhp and a top speed of 118mph, it needs a gallon of fuel every 10.7 miles, so it is perhaps no bad thing that large oil reserves are now being discovered and exploited throughout Russia.

Between 15 and 20 such cars are built each year, and sell for approximately £170,000 each.

STELA

▲ (inset) As the age old proverb (long since converted to cliché) says, necessity is the mother of invention, and this is the reason for the existence of the strange looking, two-tonne electric car from 1941 known as the STELA – an abbreviation of the manufacturing company's name.

Built in France in the early years of the Second World War, when all civilian petrol supplies had dried up, half of the car's weight was taken up by its batteries, which gave it a respectable 80 miles between charges. Petrol, however, was not the only thing in short supply, and as most of the materials needed to make such a machine became increasingly scarce production ceased after only a very few examples had been built.

Happily, this example has survived, and can be seen at the Musée Henri Malarte in Lyon, France.

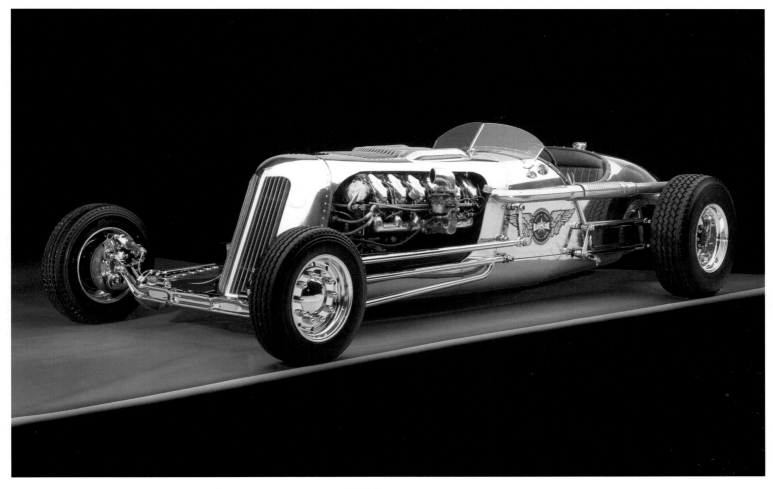

BLASTOLENE SPECIAL

▲ Just once in a while, a car comes along that is so fantastically different that it almost defies description, and it immediately burns itself into one's long-term memory banks. One such car is the Blastolene Special, a 21ft-long aluminium leviathan powered by a 29.3-litre V12 ex-Patton tank engine.

Built by Randy Grubb, the car is now owned by NBC's *Tonight Show* host and famed car collector, Jay Leno, who paid $250,000 for the one-off behemoth. The nine-tonne monster develops a staggering 810bhp, and is capable of reaching 60mph from standstill in 6.2 seconds, accompanied by the most fearsome noise, which would stir the very heart of any petrol-head. Engines of this size and power are not known for moderate thirst, however, so a fuel consumption of just 5mpg should come as no great surprise.

JET 1

◀ During the Second World War car manufacturers turned over to wartime production, and in the case of Rover this meant helping develop the first jet engines. After the war was over the company were keen to experiment further, and in 1946 set about designing a gas-turbine engine for use in a car.

By 1950 they had installed the first such engine in a highly modified P4 chassis, and after further development over the next couple of years they were ready to go public. Driven on the Jabekke highway in Belgium, in July 1952, by a very young Spen King (who later went on to design the Range Rover), it achieved 152mph.

Gas turbine engines differ from internal combustion engines in that they are very smooth due to the lack of reciprocating components, they rev at phenomenal speeds (idling at 13,000rpm), and they are rather heavy on fuel – JET 1 was able to dispose of a gallon of kerosene every four miles.

JET 1 was a national star, and when retired from PR duties was donated to the Science Museum.

CADILLAC ESCALADE

▲ The Americans have always loved big cars, and the growth of the SUV throughout the States should, in this context, come as no great surprise.

Among the biggest of the current crop of SUVs is the Cadillac Escalade, which weighs in at a portly 6,800lb. Powered by a 6-litre V8 which develops 345bhp and powers the monster truck to 60mph in under 9 seconds, its fuel consumption is not a strong point, at around 12mpg. Its list of standard fittings and options seems almost endless, and includes such useful items as a telematics system which automatically alerts emergency services in the event of an accident (providing them with the car's location), internet access, and automatic self-levelling, plus an interior festooned with more wood and cow-hide than is to be found on most ranches.

RODZILLA

▶ The Rodzilla is one of those machines that one simply has to stand back and admire. Designed in 2004 by Arizona railroad contractor Rodney Rucker, it uses a 12-cylinder, air-cooled 29.3-litre engine from a US M-47 tank that saw service in the Korean War.

Naturally, this gives the ungainly 7½ft tall behemoth a more than average turn of speed, aided and abetted by dual turbochargers force-feeding fuel into the hungry engine, which revs at less than 3,000rpm. In order to ensure this healthy performance the car has a 75-gallon fuel tank, but with a fuel consumption of almost dipsomanic proportions nothing less would suffice: expecting more than three miles per gallon can best be described as futilely optimistic.

The body perched precariously on top of the chassis is from a 1928 Studebaker and was rescued from a scrapyard, lending it the air of a machine from the classic cartoon strip 'Wacky Racers'. In truth, never was there a wackier car built; but perhaps most surprisingly of all, this car is registered and completely street-legal.

BIGFOOT

▲ To the novice, BigFoot is a one-off truck with huge wheels that goes around crushing cars and jumping over objects (including on one occasion a Boeing 727 aircraft) in stadia across the USA. There is, however, somewhat more to the BigFoot legend than this.

The latest BigFoots (not BigFeet) – there have been no less than 15 since they first appeared in 1979 – use a highly tuned 572cu in Ford engine, which develops a staggering 1,200–1,500bhp and downs up to three gallons of Methanol racing fuel in a 250yd sprint.

Costing up to $250,000 to build, the name BigFoot comes from the accusation that the car's originator kept breaking axles and engine parts by overusing his big foot.

FORD GT

◄ As a part of the company's build-up to celebrating its centenary the following year, in 2002 Ford launched an all-new, 21st-century version of their legendary supercar, the GT40, calling it the GT after being told that the name GT40 had been sold off many years previously and its new owners were asking hugely unrealistic licence fees for the new car to be allowed to use it.

Unlike the original, the 2002 car had an aluminium space frame supporting a mixture of aluminium and composite body panels, encasing a glorious 5.4-litre supercharged V8. With a top speed of 190mph and a 0–60 sprint time of 4 seconds, its performance was exactly what one would have hoped for: the 11mpg fuel consumption, however, was the price one could expect to pay when experiencing this wealth of excitement.

LAMBORGHINI MURCIELAGO

◄ Any car whose first name is Lamborghini has a duty to excel, and the Murcielago – the first Lamborghini to be designed and built under the sensible stewardship of Audi – did not disappoint.

Its top speed reaches the magic 200mph barrier, having dispensed with the first 60 in a paltry 3.8 seconds, whilst its brutal 21st-century styling reaches all the emotions touched by previous Lamborghinis. Launched in 2001 as the replacement for the much loved Diablo, lurking at the centre of this beast is a 6-litre V12 capable of delivering 580bhp, provided the delirious owner can afford to keep feeding it petrol at the depressing rate of just 11mpg. All pleasures have their price …

CHITTY CHITTY BANG BANG

◄ To most people of a certain age, the name *Chitty Chitty Bang Bang* evokes images of Dick van Dyke, flying cars, and a children's rebellion. Whilst the car in that film was a pastiche built specially for its starring role, using a Ford Zodiac V6 engine and automatic gearbox, there were three very real and terrifyingly fast cars at the beginning of the 1920s that bore the name (although not always with two Chitties in the title).

Built for Count Louis Zbrowski, a speed-loving aristocrat who spent much of his time at the famed Brooklands racing circuit in Surrey, the recipe for all three of his cars was simple: a crude, extended Edwardian chassis into which a huge aero-engine was dropped. In the case of Chitty No. 2, dating to 1922, this was an 18.9-litre six-cylinder Benz engine, which gave an impressive 230bhp and a top speed in excess of 100mph. Final drive to the rear wheels was by chain, and, as if to heighten the excitement, only the rear wheels had brakes attached to them. It may not have flown, but it would take a brave driver to hold the accelerator pedal down hard for any length of time. Fuel consumption was always in single figures.

HUMMER H1

▲ The Hummer story is an incredible one. It started out life as a crude, entirely functional piece of military hardware which, due to the likes of Arnold Schwarzeneger buying into its super-macho, flag-waving jingoism, has built up a fan base and a loyal clientele.

Its 6.5-litre, 300bhp Duramax V8 diesel engine, mated to a four-wheel-drive system, ensures that there is very little terrain over which a Hummer cannot go. Owning a Hummer makes just about the most blatant statement that ownership of any vehicle can make. Its appearance is the antithesis of automotive beauty, and is a proud boast of individuality, whilst if one needs to ask about the fuel consumption figures, 'then it ain't for you, honey.'

For many, at over $100,000 the Hummer epitomises everything that is wrong with consumerism without restraint, but to its owners a Hummer represents the ultimate in freedom to choose – choose the car, the engine, the size, the waste of resources, and to hell with the consequences.

MERCEDES-BENZ 450 SEL 6.9

◄ The Mercedes-Benz S Class, which today is renowned throughout the world as one of the finest cars available, has its roots in the W116 range 450 SEL.

The range topper was powered by a 6.9-litre dry-sump lubricated V8 which developed 286bhp, giving a 0–60 sprint time of 7.4 seconds and a top speed in excess of 140mph. Whilst these figures may not seem remarkable today, 30 years ago when the car was first launched they were enough to show a clean pair of heels to many outright sports cars of the day. Apart from its titanic levels of power, the super limousine ensured that its occupants enjoyed their journey as much as possible with the provision of a highly sophisticated suspension system, electric windows, cruise control, air-conditioning, heat-absorbing glass, head-rests etc. Naturally, all this luxury did not come cheap: its price before adding options was £22,000, less than £7,000 cheaper than the Rolls-Royce Silver Shadow II, while its ability to empty its 26-gallon fuel tanks at 11mpg was probably its least impressive trick.

JEEP HURRICANE

▼ Thinking 'outside of the box' is what concept cars are all about, but with some one is left wondering what sort of box the designer had been kept in, and for how long. One such car is 2005's Jeep Hurricane, which, apart from having the ability to turn inside its own wheelbase, or even drive sideways, has two 5.7-litre V8 Hemi engines.

The resulting 670bhp is enough to hurl the Jeep from standstill to 60mph in less than five seconds, and it has an estimated top speed of around 175mph. The left-hand pair of wheels is driven by one engine, the right-hand pair by the other. Fuel consumption figures are not quoted, but it is fair to assume that Friends of the Earth will not be joining the queue to persuade Jeep to put this particular heavy drinker into production.

BMW M5

▲ Only one event guarantees both to trouble and delight motoring journalists in equal quantities: the launch of a new BMW M5. Troubled by the lack of superlatives available to heap on the new arrival, they are simultaneously delighted by the apparent demolition of the laws of physics they experience as the new king of the road makes the planet ever smaller with its blistering speeds.

The latest M5 carries on this fine tradition, started in 1984 with the launch of the first M5. The current car boasts a full 500bhp from its V10 engine, and delivers 0–60mph in 4.6 seconds without ruffling the expensively coiffured appearance of its wealthy executive owner. The king has, however, something of a thirst, being able to drink unleaded quicker than most rugby players can quaff their favourite ales: 10.2mpg was recorded as its extra-urban consumption in an *Autocar* magazine road-test.

INTERNATIONAL CXT PICKUP

▶ The pickup is a highly usable vehicle which in recent years has developed a much higher 'cool factor' than can ever have been originally envisaged for what is essentially a utilitarian machine. With their gain in popularity, it could only ever be a matter of time before an arms race broke out between manufacturers, with each trying to build the finest, most luxurious machine, and in 2004 the International CXT was launched, immediately nuking all would-be competitors.

Built on a truck chassis, the six-tonne monster drinks a gallon of diesel every seven miles. Its 7.3-litre engine develops 220bhp, and 540lb/ft of torque, and the hubris-rig costs $93,000 in its home country, the USA.

8

SIZE ISN'T EVERYTHING ...

CLIO RENAULTSPORT V6 255

▶ It's not a new recipe, but the Clio Renaultsport V6 255 is a fantastic car nevertheless. Mimicking its predecessor, the Renault 5 Turbo, the super-Clio has had its engine taken out of its normal position and replaced by a V6 lump developing 255bhp, moved behind the seats to give the car better balance and sublime handling.

Add a set of stylish 18in OZ wheels, large frontal and rear spoilers, flared wheel-arches and sills, stiffened and lowered suspension, and large air-intakes ahead of the rear wheels, and the end result is a highly potent pocket-rocket with supercar handling, aggressive looks, and huge appeal among the *Max Power* crowd. Wild enough to enjoy on track days, its 0–60mph sprint time of under 6 seconds ensures it is also fun at the traffic lights grands prix.

NISSAN SUNNY GTI R

▼ In 1990 Nissan decided to enter rallying, and chose their newly launched Sunny as the basis for their Group A car. In standard shopping-trolley trim the Sunny was as bland as boiled potatoes, but once it had been tweaked and homologated for rally purposes it became a highly capable and entertaining car with surprisingly aggressive looks.

220bhp was now available from the turbocharged and intercooled four-cylinder 2-litre engine, giving 0–60 sprint times of just 5 seconds and a top speed of 140mph, all controlled with four-wheel drive. The agility and speed of the road cars, badged GTi R, did not translate into rally success, however, which robbed the pocket-rocket of much needed publicity, and the car's sales figures were not all that its creators might reasonably have hoped for, given its potential.

THE PINK PANTHER

▲ Whilst watching the *Pink Panther* cartoons in the 1960s was always a treat, to any self-respecting petrol-head the best bit was at the beginning, when the 26ft-long car bearing the same name, and painted in a strikingly obvious shade of pink, rolled into shot and the cartoon character leapt out. Steering the not inconsiderable bulk of the car was effected by trigger controls, the operation of which cannot have been helped by the poor field of vision on offer to the driver.

Powered by a 500bhp Chrysler V8, it was the work of Jay Ohrberg, and the rear passenger compartment featured such luxury items as a television, telephone, soda fountain, and vanity mirrors – not exactly rock'n'roll, but very Hollywood nevertheless.

LIGIER AMBRA

◄ If a principal reason behind buying a small car is cost-cutting, especially fuel-saving, then the current minuscule Ligier Ambra should appear somewhere near the top of the shopping list. Its 505cc 15bhp Lombardini diesel engine can take 85 miles to sip its way through a gallon, while the petrol version will still cover 65 miles per gallon. This parsimonious consumption enables it to get by with a fuel tank capable of holding just 17 litres (less than four gallons), adding cheap fill-ups to the joys of ownership.

Furthermore, because of its low weight and engine capacity the plastic-bodied two-seater is classified as a quadricycle, which means it can be driven in the UK by a 17-year-old with just a motorcycle licence rather than a full car licence.

MYCAR

▶ MyCar is a city car, whose top speed is just a shade over 50mph. Power is available from a variety of air-cooled petrol engines located at the rear, ranging from 50cc to 250cc, and an electric version is also available. Its minuscule appearance is aimed at appealing to the young at heart with the added bonus of not requiring a large parking spot.

Luxuries beyond a connection for an MP3 reader, a storage net, and seat-belts are somewhat thin on the ground, but in its favour the hard-top roof is easily removed to turn it into an open-topped cabriolet, giving it the feeling of a sports car, if not the performance.

FUBAR FACTORY HOPPA

▼ When the flower-power generation of the late 1960s started customising VW Beetles and turning them into Beach Buggies, the cars they built were fun cars. The Fubar Factory Hoppa is a 21st-century interpretation of this theme – except that in place of the VW floorpan there is now a tubular steel space-frame chassis, and instead of a wheezing old Beetle lump designed before the Second World War there is a 2-litre Subaru Imprezza engine, and a five-speed gearbox.

The occupants also have something more raw to smile about than each other's clothes and hairstyles. A top speed comfortably in the hundred-plus zone, with the first 60mph being passed in 4.5 seconds, is startling performance for a design which owes much more to the necessities of fun cruising than the disciplines of a wind-tunnel, and gives ample justification for its manufacturers referring to it as a 'Son of a Beach Street Buggy'.

AUSTIN SE7EN

◀ Usually when manufacturers use what appears to be a deliberate mistake in a car's name it is safe to assume that this has been done to distract attention from a desperately dull vehicle. In the case of the 1959 Austin Se7en, or Mini as it was subsequently to become known, this was far from the case.

Famously designed by Alex Issigonis, many people believe it was the first car to have front-wheel drive and the engine located transversely, but this honour actually goes to the 1946 Lloyd 650. The Mini was, however, a car of unparalleled simplicity and purity of design: it was right in almost every way, although it was not an immediate sales success.

Management at the Ford Motor Company saw the threat this car posed to their own line-up but could not work out how BMC were able to make it for the money, so they bought one, took it to pieces, and cost-analysed it before arriving at the startling conclusion that BMC were actually losing £30 on each Mini they built. Ford therefore decided not to try and compete with the Mini but instead launched the Cortina, which was a big car offered at the price of a small one.

AUBURN 851 SPEEDSTER

▼ The straight-eight supercharged Auburn 851 Speedster of 1935 was a most flamboyant car, whose styling was the handiwork of Gordon Buehrig. It looked streamlined and super-fast, which it was – every car was tested by racing driver Ab Jenkins before it left the factory, and was guaranteed to be capable of more than 100mph from the day its customer bought it. A plaque was fitted to the dash with Jenkins's autograph engraved next to the speed he had achieved in that particular vehicle on its test run.

150bhp was extracted from the 4.6-litre side-valve engine with the help of a Schwitzer Cummins Supercharger, and although it was capable of these high speeds it was expected to spend much more time as a pose machine with its rich and glamorous owner rather than tearing up roads. This particular example was owned by Marlene Dietrich and featured in the film *Desire*. The car is on permanent display at the National Motor Museum, Beaulieu.

In spite of its lines and enormous size, luggage space was inordinately small: just enough room was provided through a hatch behind the cabin for one set of golf clubs.

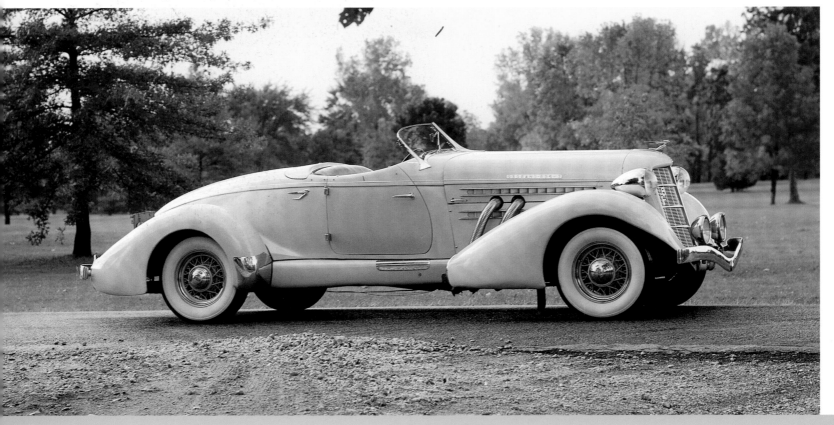

PEUGEOT 205 T16

▲ The name Jean Todt is now famous for leading the Ferrari F1 team to a string of consecutive World Championships, but before he made the switch to Formula 1 he had already made a considerable name for himself in rallying. The fearsome Group B Peugeot 205 T16, for instance, which externally resembled the front-wheel-drive family hatchback but underneath the skin was a very different animal, was conceived by Todt.

Four-wheel drive gave the levels of grip required, while the 1,800cc four-cylinder engine received extra urge from a turbocharger, and in road-trim developed 200bhp in its new location behind the seats. A top speed of 130mph brought plenty of smiles to the faces of the 200 owners quick enough to snap up one of these rare supercars when they were launched in 1983, and once Peugeot had made the regulation number for homologation purposes no more road cars were built.

The Evolution versions, destined for the hands of aces such as Ari Vatanen and Juha Kankunnen, were highly successful in a number of rallies, adding further colour to what many regard as a golden age of the sport.

SCAMP ROWFANT

▶ There are many people for whom the appeals of the old Suzuki SJ 413 wannabe Jeep do not work, and for such people there is a car that uses the oily bits of said Japanese mini mud-plugger to great effect. That car is the Rowfant of 2000, a strange blend of 4x4 and pseudo-vintage tourer.

Sold as a kit, once the builder has had the pleasure of removing another SJ 413 from the roads permanently and got rid of all the bodywork, the chassis is sent off to Scamp, the manufacturers of the kit, for modification, and upon its return the creative process is relatively straightforward. The end result, depending to a certain extent on the skill and budget of the kit's builder, is a highly distinctive vehicle, with the looks of a shrunken 1930s car and the ability to haul itself through some very muddy places.

AIXAM 500 EVOLUTION

▶ Just how small can a car be made that will carry four people in safety and some degree of comfort? Judging by the Aixam 500 Evolution (almost sounds sporty, doesn't it?), launched in 1995, a mite under 9ft in length seems about right.

The number 500 in its name refers to the (rounded-up) engine size: 479cc of twin-cylinder diesel excitement is transmitted to the front wheels by an idiot-proof infinitely variable automatic gearbox with one forward and one reverse gear, so a career in racing seems unlikely for the diminutive French car. 70mpg, however, makes amends for the lack of oomph, whilst levels of luxury are extraordinarily high for a car in this class: electric windows, central-locking, metallic paint, cigar lighter, alloy wheels, and even wood effect veneer on the dashboard, are all available to would-be owners to persuade them that whilst the performance is lacklustre, it is still better than travelling on a bus.

NISSAN HYPERMINI

▲ At the beginning of the 21st century, much of the world is finally awakening to the fact that fossil fuel sources are not limitless, and serious steps are being taken to find alternatives. With cities becoming gridlocked by the ever-increasing number of cars entering them, this is another issue that is being faced by responsible manufacturers.

Enter, in 1999, the Nissan Hypermini, a two-seater that not only uses no fossil fuel (apart from that consumed by the power-plant that supplies the electricity to charge its batteries), but is small enough to occupy much less space than most other cars. Being electrically powered, its anticipated primary use is in the city, where it can go up to 100 miles between charges, and it has a top speed of 60mph should road conditions allow. As with many similar electric superminis, as yet it does not offer quite the same freedom as a petrol car can, but within its limitations it can be seen as a viable alternative to some journeys.

ITALDESIGN BIGA

▲ The Biga was a strange little machine designed at the beginning of the 1990s by Giugiaro for Italdesign, and first shown at the 1992 Turin Motorshow.

Measuring just 2m in length, the diminutive little hybrid diesel-electric-powered car was aimed at city authorities who would purchase fleets of them and then make them available to participants in the scheme, who would rent them by the hour and pay by a credit card system. Its bodywork was made from fibreglass, with a single, rear door, and whilst purposeful and – due to its minuscule size – making little impact on its surroundings, it could never be accused of possessing good looks.

The idea went no further than producing the one example.

REVA CLASSIC

▲ The number of times a car manufacturer has boasted that 'The car of tomorrow is here today' as they point beamingly at their latest model is huge, and one of the latest to make this boast is Reva, India's first electric car company. Whilst it cannot, in all truth, claim to have conquered the well-known problems of electric cars, an electric car is a definite step in the right direction for the streets of India's heavily polluted cities.

The Reva Classic is a miniature two-door fun car, with a range of 50 miles, and needs eight hours for the batteries to recharge. The dinky little bodywork is made from ABS (Acrylonitrile Butadine Styrene), which is a dent- and scratch-resistant plastic and comes in any one of 2,000 colours, which means you really *can* have exactly the colour scheme you want.

FORD ZODIAC MK IV

▲ Still sporting fins at the rear, by 1965 Ford's ageing Mk III Zodiac was looking way past its sell-by date, and its replacement needed to do some serious catching up in the style stakes. The Mk IV had very different lines, and with its huge size certainly grabbed attention wherever it went. Costing less than £1,250 at launch, including purchase tax, this was certainly a lot of car for the money, and the subsequently launched Executive model carried even more prestige, with leather upholstery and a sunroof as well as a bonnet mascot similar to that fitted to Lincolns.

Its top speed of just over 100mph from its 3-litre V6 was adequate, but noted saloon-racing champion Sir John Whitmore loathed it, especially its handling, and branded it, perhaps a little unkindly, 'the flying pig'. His scathing comments do not appear to have damaged the sales prospects of this enormous upper-management status car, however, as nearly 50,000 examples sold during its five years in production.

VIGNALE GAMINE

◄ One must assume that Senor Vignale was unfamiliar with Enid Blyton's tales of Noddy and Big Ears, as the Gamine – which he designed on the chassis of the tiny Fiat 500, and to which he gave his name – bore a striking resemblance to Noddy's car.

Quite why, in 1967, he elected to throw away the bodywork of the Fiat, which many believe to be something of an automotive masterpiece, in favour of this shambolic convertible complete with fake radiator grille (which it didn't need, as the engine was at the rear anyway) is a question that will never be satisfactorily answered. Several hundred were imported into the UK during its three-year lifespan, but, in common with Fiats of the time, the British climate proved to be their downfall: rust readily ate away at the little oddity, and today very few remain.

PURE BRILLIANCE

LOTUS 340R

◄ The 340R was an extreme development of the fabulously successful Elise, and its design was aided by various staff members of *Autocar* magazine at the invitation of Lotus chief Chris Knight. When Lotus had launched the Elise, many may have thought that it was a stripped-to-basics racer, but the 340R showed how much more could still be removed, and how aggressive the little rocket could become.

Launched in 1999, it sold at the bargain price of £35,000, and just 340 examples were built. There was no choice of colour scheme – black and silver or nothing – and the only option available was an anti-theft alarm system. It used the 1.8-litre Rover K series engine tuned to deliver 177bhp to give it a 0–60mph sprint time of 4.3 seconds and a top speed of 130mph, and the press loved it.

JAGUAR XK120

► The Earls Court Motor Show of 1948 was the first such event held in the UK since the outbreak of war in 1939, and most of the cars on display were pretty similar to those that had been on sale before the war. The country's economy was spluttering back into life, but designing cars takes time, and the number of genuinely new cars on display was not great.

Among those on show for the first time, however, was the Jaguar XK120, a shape so swoopingly beautiful it immediately stole the limelight. Not only was its bodywork stunningly modern, but it was also very fast, and had under its slender bonnet the world's first production twin cam engine.

Living up to the qualities of its namesake from the animal kingdom, the Jaguar was exceptionally agile and fast in the right hands. It won many rallies and races, and came very close to a win at Le Mans in 1951.

BENZ 3-WHEELER

◄ Karl Benz, the son of a steam engineer, had trained as a watch mechanic, and in the early 1880s was working in a firm making stationary engines when he became increasingly caught up with the idea of developing a horse-free means of road transport. Steam engines had been used to power railway locomotives for over 75 years by then, but were too big and heavy to be of use for road vehicles: Benz knew that something rather different would be needed if Dobbin and his many friends were ever to be able to look forward to retirement.

He set about trying to make an engine small enough, light enough, and yet with enough power to propel a vehicle, reasoning that the best way of achieving these goals was to build a small four-stroke engine that could run on petrol rather than coal gas, as the liquid fuel would be easier to carry on board and had more explosive power.

The engine was capable of 0.75hp from its 954cc single cylinder, which drove a large horizontal flywheel. In 1885 he put it in a lightweight tube chassis with just one wheel at the front and power delivered to the rear wheels by means of a flat leather band. Crude it most definitely was, but it worked, and it was the very first car, from which all subsequent variants can rightly be said to have evolved.

GIBBS HUMDINGA

◀ It's probably fair to say that most people don't regularly need to travel at 100mph on land and 40mph on water in the same vehicle, but for those who do there is now, finally, an answer: the Gibbs Humdinga, launched (literally) in 2004.

Powered by a 350-bhp engine, this huge machine is capable of carrying five people, and can transform from high speed car to speedboat in a few seconds. Once in the water, the wheels retract and the power train switches from wheels to jet propulsion, which enables the Humdinga's not inconsiderable size to plane across the water's surface at a truly exhilarating rate of knots.

CITROËN SM

▼ A Citroën powered by a Maserati engine sounds like the sort of thing a Parisian customiser might build to impress his friends, but in 1970 this was a real car, on sale at Citroën main dealers. At that time the French firm were the owners of Maserati, and having no six-cylinder engines in their own line-up they decided to borrow the 2,670cc V6 170bhp engine from the Merak and put it into a Citroën DS-inspired chassis, and clothe it in a super-slippery two-door four-seater coupé body.

The result was the SM, which had a top speed of 135mph and a variety of novel features, such as six headlights, two of which turned with the steering so as to light corners more effectively. It was also blessed with the legendary ride quality of the DS, whilst its steering was lightning quick, with just two turns from lock to lock. Among Citroën fans the SM is still talked of in hushed tones of reverence, even though the car never made the company any money. It was killed off in 1975 by the fuel crisis after just 12,290 examples had been built.

BUGATTI VEYRON

▶ To be able to boast that your company builds the fastest car in the world is an unattainable dream for most. Jaguar managed it for a very short time with their XJ220, until the McLaren F1 wrested it from them; and McLaren in turn have recently lost it to the 9F-V400.

The latter's days of kingship could nevertheless be severely limited, as Volkswagen, of all companies – the people's car company, and owner of the Bugatti name – aim to be the next holder of this trophy, with the new ultimate in ultra-fast cars, the Veyron. Powered by a 1,001bhp W16, quad-turbo, 8-litre engine located behind the passenger cell, the four-wheel-drive masterpiece is claimed to have a top speed of a full 252mph. The first 186mph will be reached in just 14 seconds. Launch has been delayed several times while problems with dispersing engine heat are solved and perfection is achieved in areas such as refinement and luxury, but once launched this new piece of automotive art is likely to assume the title of the fastest production car ever.

SAAB 91

▼ The Saab 91 was launched on 10 June 1947 as the first car from a Swedish firm more normally associated with aeroplane manufacture. Work on it had begun almost two years previously, and what the assembled public and journalists were looking at was the prototype for the subsequent 92 model.

Whilst the 92 was not necessarily to everyone's taste, the 91, with its two-stroke two-cylinder engine capable of a top speed of 62mph, was a stunning shape which even today still looks strikingly modern and beautifully aerodynamic. One might perhaps expect something aerodynamic from a company that had several decades of aircraft-building experience, but making something with such lasting appeal is no small achievement, and was a particularly fine way of starting a car company.

PURE BRILLIANCE

JAGUAR XK180

▲ The Jaguar XK180 was a truly beautiful design study launched in 1997 to universal acclaim, immediately re-igniting talk among press and enthusiasts about the possibility of a forthcoming F Type successor to the long-dead E Type.

Whilst it was obvious that the svelte lines would never make it to production unaltered, the hope was that the love-at-first-sight reactions of all and sundry would force Jaguar to consider making a full production version based on this most handsome of roadsters. Fitted with a supercharged and inter-cooled version of the AJ V8 engine tuned up to 450bhp, the car was created by taking out 5in from the chassis of a production version XKR, and then clothing it in hand-rolled aluminium panels, working to drawings by Jaguar Styling Department's chief stylist, Keith Helfet.

Unfortunately, beautiful though it was, it heralded nothing more than yet another false dawn for the mythical F Type, which still exists only in the wishful thinking of Jaguar enthusiasts around the globe.

BENTLEY 4½-LITRE SUPERCHARGED

▼ The story of Bentleys at Le Mans during the 1920s is the stuff of legend, as Bentley reigned absolutely supreme at the French track for much of the decade.

The 4½-litre supercharged Bentley, introduced in 1929, was the fastest of them all with a top speed of 120mph, but due to unreliability it never joined the ranks of its forebears with a win at the famous French race. Resplendent in its British Racing Green paint, with the huge supercharger mounted below the massive radiator and Union Jack badges on its flanks, it is a powerful image of pre-war British pride, whilst its interior lacks any of the later trappings of luxury, with a string-bound steering wheel so huge it would look more at home on a boat, and a turned aluminium dash with gauges and oil feeds liberally dotted around.

CITROËN 2CV

▶ Whilst there will undoubtedly be those who fail to see anything brilliant in the hippie's favourite, the Citroën 2CV, there are many others who feel it was one of the most important cars of the 20th century, every bit as important as the Ford Model T, and its simple design with incredible strengths show signs of genius missing from cars many times more complex and expensive.

At launch in 1949, the spartan front-wheel-drive car came with a 375cc engine that gave 9hp and a top speed of just under 40mph. What it lacked in performance, however, it more than compensated for in ride comfort, space, and sheer usability – plus, of course, it had a full-length fabric sunroof for those long summer days.

As cheap transport it had few equals, and was a huge success. Performance figures usually required measuring with an hourglass rather than a stopwatch, but later models came with a 602cc engine which allowed slightly more acceptable progress.

FERRARI DAYTONA

▼ Known officially as the GTB/4, the Ferrari Daytona is largely regarded as one of the finest cars the marque has ever produced. It was the last front-engined V12 Ferrari, and cognoscenti will add that it was also the last Ferrari to be built without any Fiat influence.

Its 4.4-litre twin overhead cam V12 gave 352bhp, a top speed of 175mph, 0–60 in 5.3 seconds, and a noise to die for. These figures from a road-going car at the beginning of the 1970s were startling enough, but its delicious styling, a work of genius from Pininfarina, ensured that this was a car with almost universal appeal and cachet.

Available as either a coupé, or in GTS/4 form as a Berlinetta Spyder (roadster), the car was sold over a four-year period that ended in 1974, and today genuine examples with good provenance command enormous prices.

ASTON MARTIN DBR9GT

▲ The car manufacturing business can be a roller coaster of a ride, as Aston Martin know only too well. At the beginning of the 1990s they were languishing (in 1993 they sold only 43 cars), somehow just managing to stay alive as they had for much of the company's lifespan, when over the hill rode the cavalry, wearing blue oval badges that read 'Ford'.

Since then the company has gone from strength to strength, and the latest and most ebullient display of this confidence is the £475,000, 600bhp, carbon-fibre and aluminium super-monster that is the DBR9GT. This ultra-car – to call it a supercar seems almost demeaning – is the brainchild of the company's CEO, Dr Ulrich Bez, whose aim is to see the company reclaim some of its past Le Mans glory.

With most cars the 0–60mph sprint is important, and the DBR9GT can accomplish this in 3.9 seconds, but the 6.5 seconds it takes to reach 100mph tells a fuller story of this car's huge power, and illustrates what life on the far side of 200mph is like.

DUESENBERG MODEL J

◄ The Duesenberg Model J of 1928–36 was a prince among cars admired and appreciated around the world. Fitted with a straight-eight 6.8-litre engine that developed 265bhp, it was capable of 116mph. Each chassis was tested for 500 miles around the Indianapolis racetrack before being handed over to a coachbuilder to be fitted with the chosen bodywork of its new owner.

Apart from the arrestingly beautiful coachwork that complemented the quality of the mechanicals, there were many things to recommend this highly expensive icon of success. One such detail, of which many will be unaware, was the timing-box fitted to all cars, which alerted the owner to the need for an oil-change every time a further 700 miles had been clocked up, and even operated a pump every 75 miles which greased all the lubrication points on the chassis.

Owned when new by film stars such as Greta Garbo and Mae West, today they are prized exhibits in many of the world's finest car collections and museums.

JENSEN FF INTERCEPTOR

▶ Introduced at the London Motorshow in 1966, the Jensen FF Interceptor was not just a very handsome car, courtesy of its Vignale styling: it was also a new British supercar, albeit powered by a 6,276cc V8 from Chrysler in the US. As was to be expected, all the usual qualities associated with a hand-built British aristo-car were there in spadefuls.

Its ability to reach 100mph in 19 seconds from standstill and a top speed of 135mph was also worthy of note, but the use of the 'Ferguson Formula' four-wheel-drive system was not only revolutionary thinking almost a decade-and-a-half ahead of the Audi Quattro, but when mated to the Dunlop Maxaret anti-lock braking system it marked the FF out as a truly innovative car.

The cost of this extra safety, however, was an additional £1,500 over the price of an Interceptor, which resulted in slow sales, and the FF was killed off after selling just 320 examples.

FERRARI F430 SPIDER

▲ One task in which Ferrari has almost always succeeded is raising the expectations of the motoring world, and with the arrival of its 2005 F430 Spider the list of jobs well done by the Maranello firm grew by one.

With very few exceptions, Ferraris have always been supremely elegant and continually redefine our perceptions of design excellence, and the F430 Spider is no exception. Add to good looks performance figures of 0–60mph in 4.5 seconds and a top speed of 200mph from its 490bhp 4.3-litre V8, whose musical howl is all the more audible with the hood down, and the recipe for automotive pure love is written large in carbon-fibre and metal, painted blood red and adorned with a prancing horse emblem on its rear. Again.

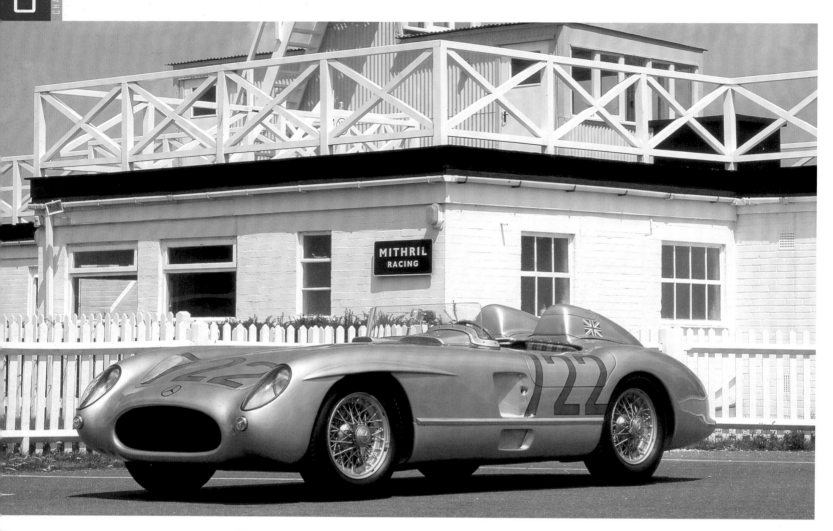

MERCEDES-BENZ 300 SLR

▲ In 1955 high tech came no higher than the Mercedes-Benz 300 SLR, about which rumour spread for a short while that a customer version might be offered in strictly limited numbers.

For wealthy sports car fans, such a possibility must have induced huge amounts of salivating, as here was a car that had finished in first place in five of the first six races it entered, including the gruelling Mille Miglia, in the hands of Stirling Moss. Powered by a 3-litre V8 that developed an astounding 310bhp, it was capable of speeds of up to 186mph, reaching its first 60mph from standstill in just 7 seconds. In 1955, these figures, which even today are pretty impressive, must have been barely credible. The car never made it into road-car production trim: the few that were built and survive therefore command astronomical prices in keeping with their legendary status.

FERRARI 250 GTO

◄ It is all but impossible to quantify what exactly it is that elevates the 250 GTO above all other Ferraris and to the stratosphere of ultimate desirability, but there is an undeniable magic about the car. In comparing it to a work of art (and this book would certainly not be the first so to do), its equivalent would be the Venus de Milo, but complete with arms.

Its 3-litre V12 sings a more tuneful note than the great Pavarotti could ever hope to muster, as it summons its 300bhp to launch the masterpiece towards its top speed of over 150mph. It is impossible to see how its sensuous shape could be improved, whilst its pace and stability on the racetrack made it the most successful GT racer of the early 1960s. Only 39 were ever built (between 1962 and 1963), and on the very rare occasions that one changes hands the asking price is many millions.

ASTON MARTIN DB5

▲ An interesting question worthy of an essay on a car design course is 'Would the Aston Martin DB5 be held in the high esteem it enjoys without the numbers 007 forever associated with it?' The simple fact is, that no other car would have been right for a character whose principal characteristic was his innate Englishness.

Even the company's name is double-barrelled, and every line of the DB5 epitomises the air of an English gentleman. Built between 1963 and 1965, its 282bhp, 4-litre straight six engine purred with perfection and delivered a top speed of 141mph with consummate ease. Hand-built quality was visible everywhere on the 1,022 examples built, and the high rate of survival is further testament to the unique appeal of this most special of sports cars.

VOLKSWAGEN GOLF GTI MK 1

▶ May 1974 must have been a tense time in Wolfsburg: VW Group had shown a loss in their accounts for the first time ever, and they were replacing the Beetle with a car so entirely different that being nervous was entirely forgivable.

They needn't have worried, however, as the Giugiaro-designed Golf was a masterpiece. The following September, reluctantly, VW management sanctioned the building of 5,000 go-faster versions to homologate the car for Group 1 racing. Badged as a GTi, this was a new direction for VW. Its fuel-injected 1,588cc engine gave 110bhp and a top speed of 112mph, which was considered a highly useful turn of speed in the mid-seventies.

Uncomplicated, superbly agile, and enormous fun, the Golf GTi was an immediate success, and can rightly be seen as the true father of the phenomenon known as the 'hot-hatch'. Subsequent editions have been faster, and better equipped, but none have managed to recapture the sheer right-ness of the 1975 original.

LOTUS CORTINA MK1

◄ The Mk1 Cortina was a light and very strong car, and as such was almost bound to appeal to the go-faster wizard of the 1960s, Colin Chapman. The Lotus Cortina was a happy marriage between Chapman, who was always keen to build the fastest cars for racing, and Ford of Britain, who had decided that motorsport was a good way to attract publicity and sell cars.

The Lotus version of the family car differed in various steel body panels being replaced with aluminium, in having stiffened front suspension and a new rear diff and suspension (which proved fragile), and in the installing of the glorious twin-cam Lotus engine, which gave it a top speed of 108mph, reaching the first 60mph in 10 seconds. On the racetracks it was king, and in the hands of drivers such as Jim Clark and Sir John Whitmore was pure magic to watch.

FORD SIERRA RS 500 COSWORTH

►Hooligan cars are nearly always fun, and some of the finest hooligan cars over the years have worn the familiar blue oval badge proudly on their bonnets.

The 1987 Ford Sierra RS500 Cosworth (the number refers to the number built, not the bhp count) ranks among the finest in this category. Built on the three-door family hatchback bodyshell, it shared very little else with its humble brother. It was put together by Aston Martin Tickford, in a factory near Coventry, and its primary purpose, as far as Ford were concerned, was to achieve wins in the various forms of motorsport it entered: in race trim, with 550bhp available, it was unbeatable. The de-tuned road vehicles, with 224bhp available to them, were aggressive looking wild cars, with huge coffee-table spoilers on the boot, and had a top speed of more than 150mph, reaching the first 60 in just 6.2 seconds once the rear wheels, which did all the driving, had managed to grip the tarmac.

Being rear-wheel drive made the RS500 more entertaining than many of its performance contemporaries, and it is highly prized today as one of the great go-faster cars of the 1980s.

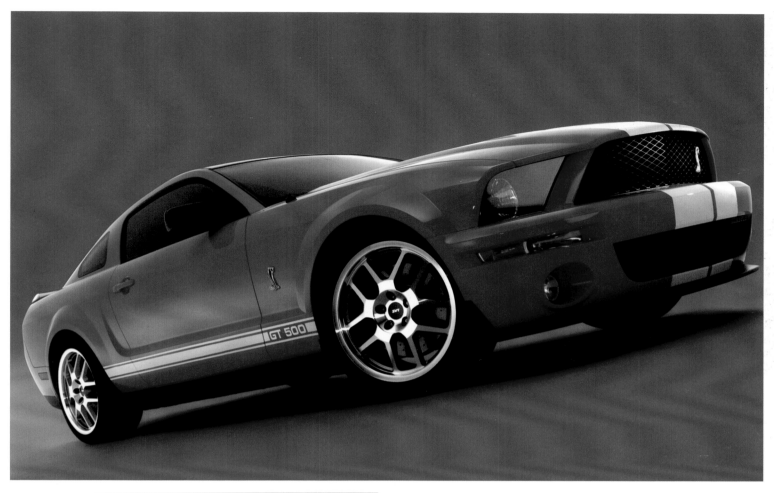

FORD SHELBY MUSTANG COBRA GT500

▲ Carroll Shelby is a name forever linked with the growling super muscle-car of the 1960s, the Cobra. It has now been resurrected and added to the name of Ford Mustang GT500 to give a thoroughly confusing mouthful.

Hugely aggressive, this monster is a modern interpretation and combination of the sporting heritage of two classics. Its 450bhp V8 is mated to a six-speed manual transmission, and unashamedly harks back to the glory days of the Cobras and Mustangs. Inside, the cabin is trimmed in red leather, and titanium-faced gauges await the eager driver, whilst the exterior sports Le Mans racing stripes, 19in alloy wheels, and a variety of aerodynamic enhancements to distinguish it from lesser models.

BENTLEY CONTINENTAL FLYING SPUR

◄ The launch of a new Bentley saloon is a pretty rare occasion: ignoring those based on Rolls-Royce models, approximately seven-and-a-half decades had passed between the last such launch and the arrival in 2005 of the new Continental Flying Spur, and whilst this is an inordinately long time it would appear that the wait was worthwhile.

Its 552bhp 6-litre twin-turbocharged engine drives all four wheels, and has taken from the Vauxhall Lotus Carlton the title of fastest four-door saloon in the world, with a top speed of 208mph, as verified by some highly delighted *Autocar* journalists. As one would expect, the level of luxury is unsurpassed, with 11 cows giving their hides to clothe the interior, alongside some of the finest wood veneer work ever, and every conceivable creature comfort has been designed into the new car.

Whilst a price tag of more than £115,000 can never be called cheap, in relative terms, and considering the amount of technology, beauty, and kudos that comes with this new super-saloon, the Bentley Continental Flying Spur – a name last used by Bentley in the 1950s – offers a lot of car for the money.

10

VISIONS OF THE FUTURE

VOLVO 3CC

► What differentiates the 2004 Volvo 3CC from many other show cars is that it represents more than the wishful thinking of a few designers encouraged by an eager Marketing Department: it is the result of detailed and advanced research, and there is much in it which will see production reality in the not very distant future.

Its striking shape is the first thing one notices, and this is the result of a new 2+1 seating arrangement. It has the dimensions of a small sports car and yet it can carry more people. Of greater significance is the way that the seats all move forwards on shock absorbers in the event of an accident, which helps dissipate the energy and reduce possible injuries. Powered by electricity, it can reach 60mph in 10 seconds and has a top speed of 85mph, which it can achieve with zero emissions.

Future cars may not all look like this, but they will work similarly to it.

FRAZER NASH SOLAR BABY 2

▼ The name Frazer Nash is most readily associated with pre-war chain-driven sports cars, but more recently the firm has turned its revitalised energies to planet-saving electric cars, such as the challenging Solar Baby 2.

Its makers refer to it as an Urban Transporter, which may sound like the Marketing Department trying to reinvent the car (rather than merely the wheel), but in truth, so different is it from any car currently available that perhaps this apparent conceit is permissible. Naturally, given its power source, it boasts zero emissions (at least from the car, if not the power station that generates the electricity stored in its batteries), but it also boasts a luxury interior and minimal maintenance as other selling points, alongside its totally unique appearance.

MDI AIRCAR

▲ Finding an alternative fuel to power our cars has taxed the brains of our brightest scientists for more than a generation, and while many have come up with clever suggestions none come close to the 21st-century solution put forward by MDI, who have invented an engine that runs on compressed air.

A number of what can most charitably be called quirky designs have been built around the engine, such as the taxi pictured here, which can run up to 180 miles on a tank of compressed air, with a top speed of almost 70mph. Recharging the tank can take four hours from a mains-powered compressor, or just three minutes at an air-station, whilst the options include having airbags fitted – although these are presumably not fed from the car's 'fuel' tank.

LUNAR ROVER

▲ Almost certainly the most expensive car ever built (five were built at a total cost in 1970 of $38,000,000), the Lunar Rover had the sort of performance most writers would describe as miserable. Its top speed of just 11mph was achieved with the help of an electric motor in each wheel, powered by two 36-volt silver-zinc batteries that gave it a range of 40 miles.

It was subjected to a strict weight cutting programme that most F1 teams would be familiar with, and when even tyres were deemed too heavy they were replaced with wire mesh doughnuts held on with circular bracing, all of which helped achieve the impressive weight of just 210kg unladen. Whilst four made a one-way journey to the moon, the fifth example is owned by the Smithsonian Institute.

BUICK LE SABRE

◀ Many of the most striking designs to come out of the American motor industry during the 1950s were either the work of, or influenced by, one man: Harley Earl. One of his early and truly visionary designs was the Buick Le Sabre of 1951, a concept marketed as 'an experimental laboratory on wheels'

We are nowadays familiar with concept cars that promise fantasy motoring, but in 1951 the concept car was still in its infancy, and on the Le Sabre all the gadgets worked. One of these was a rain sensor which, when activated, automatically raised the roof and windows if the car was parked with the top down. Other gadgets included built-in jacks and the world's first wrap-around curved windscreen. Powered by a 335bhp V8 engine, this high-tech car — much of which was built from magnesium, aluminium and glass-fibre — was a stunner, which even today still wows onlookers.

VAUXHALL SRV

▲ Back in 1974, the SRV from Vauxhall was seen by hopefuls as the sort of car we might all be driving today. In spite of its incredibly low profile of just 41in this was a full four-seater, and it was loaded with ground-breaking ideas, many of which have not as yet been incorporated into real-world car design.

One such idea was the ability to trim its aerodynamic profile when travelling at speed, using an aerofoil in the nose, electric levelling at the rear, and the ability to redistribute the fuel load around the car by pumping it into a number of tanks. Other features included fixed seating while the steering wheel and pedals were movable, and having all the instrumentation and controls located in a pod hinged on the driver's door.

Entry into and exit from a car so low is not easy, however, and one can only imagine that the designers believed that by the time it became an everyday vehicle on the world's roads arthritis and other mobility-restricting diseases would have been eradicated. We are still waiting.

TH!NK CITY

▲ Whilst the Pink Panther might have told us to 'Think Pink' at the start of his cartoon programmes, engineers in Oslo at the end of the last century were very much hoping the good citizens of that most pretty of places would TH!NK electric.

This cute little plastic-bodied city car was powered by nickel cadmium batteries which gave it a range of between 50 and 90 miles between charges and a top speed of almost 60mph. Charge time from flat was around eight hours, which could be achieved at home by simply plugging it into the mains, or at various charge-points around the city.

Although feasible as a city car, ultimately the TH!NK did not provide the great leap forwards that parent company Ford had been hoping for, and after several years during which it was shown at motor shows around the globe, the decision was taken to concentrate on fuel cell research, and the project was wound up in 2002.

ISUZU KAI

▼ Although we are not expected to take some of the wilder concept cars as much more than idle fancies aimed at attracting headlines and attention, it is hard to accept that a company would spend the considerable sums involved in developing these cars without hoping either to explore new design avenues or more importantly to clinic such ideas to see whether the public find them appealing.

So what are we to make of the Isuzu Kai? Launched in 2000, it is a fantastically butch, modernist 4x4/family car crossover, which appears to be the handiwork of someone addicted to Pokemon-style cartoons. Powered by a 3-litre V6 diesel engine mated to an automatic gearbox, its brutal styling will not be to everyone's taste, and whilst such features as the suicide rear doors and awkward detailing such as the rectangular rear wheel-arches will not see production reality, one can expect to see such crossovers become increasingly common in the future.

INVICTA S1

▲ More than six decades after the last new Invicta rolled off a production line, the name was resurrected and given to a car that could easily claim to be in the same mould as its previous proud bearers, this time coming from deepest Wiltshire and costing a very 21st-century £69,950.

The price, however, was not the only modern element to the car unveiled at the 2002 British Motor Show. Its svelte body was built from carbon-fibre bonded to a steel tube space-frame chassis, and with its rear wheels powered by a 320bhp 4.6-litre V8 it was capable of 170mph.

The manufacturers proudly boast that it was designed to be two cars in one – a luxurious Grand Tourer in the Invicta tradition and a no-compromise sports car able to race to 60mph in 5 seconds, on its way to a 170mph maximum.

SOCEMA-GREGOIRE

▼ The search for alternatives to the internal combustion engine is not new, and throughout the entire history of the car there are littered examples, mostly failures, of attempts to overthrow the supremacy of the petrol engine. In the 1950s gas turbines seemed a promising way to go, and Rover's JET 1 reached speeds of more than 150mph in 1952 powered by this type of engine.

Simultaneous to the development of the Rover, the incredibly slippery (cd of 0.19) Socema-Gregoire was being readied to wow the crowds at the 1952 Paris Salon – a feat it excelled in with its Buck Rogers coachwork and the promise of high-tech, high glamour high speeds.

Unfortunately it was not to be, as management changes at parent company CEM saw the project ditched before the car had a chance to prove itself, although in fairness it was doubted that it could match the speeds attained by the Rover anyway. The only example still exists, happily, and can be seen at the Le Mans motor museum with just 27km recorded on its odometer.

FORD FX ATMOS

▲ The 1950s were a great time for believing in the future. Scientists were seen as visionaries in whom we could all place our trust, and each new invention would make our lives that little bit better, before we all set off to live in colonies on the moon.

Concept car designers of the time had free range to explore the full depths of their sci-fi imaginations, and one product of this era of unbridled optimism was the FX Atmos from Ford. With its rocket-inspired styling, glass canopy, and huge fins, it was obvious that this would be one of the last cars to be built for use on this planet, as it appeared reasonably well equipped for space travel. One innovation which may have been of more use than the pedestrian-unfriendly spikes protruding from the car's front was the 'Roadarscope', which was supposed to be an autopilot, allowing the driver time away from the controls so that he could slip into a sparkly silver space-suit en route to his next engagement.

As yet, few of the futuristic features of the FX Atmos have made it into production.

CADILLAC SIXTEEN

▼ The Cadillac Sixteen is a concept car, launched in 2004, which, in spite of the world's growing energy crisis, boasts an astounding 13.6-litre V16 engine that delivers 1,000bhp.

As is so often the case with concept cars, however, if one looks below the surface things are not as alarming as at first appears, since whilst the headline figures of 1,000bhp are accurate, the engine, through clever electronic trickery, is able to run on as few as four cylinders when the power is not required, and can therefore, theoretically, go some way to justifying itself in the 21st century. Clever electronics also control the systems which steer all four of its 24in polished aluminium wheels, whilst inside hand-woven silk carpets, Tuscany leather seating, a Bose sound system, and a DVD information and entertainment system await future owners should the car ever proceed beyond the concept stage.

BERTONE STRATOS ZERO

▶ Visitors to the 1970 Turin Motor Show had an enormous surprise waiting for them. There, for the first time, was the Bertone Stratos Zero, a concept car that looked like it was not so much from another century, more from another planet.

Powered by a 2.4-litre V6 placed amidships, it was capable of 120mph, but its spaceship lines made it look like intergalactic travel was more on the menu than mere road transport. At just 44in high, its razor-sharp profile was a real head-turner, with an interior every bit as futuristic as the exterior.

Entry was not easy, visibility was almost non-existent, and practicality was something of an alien concept, but much of the car, including the majority of its wedgy profile, nevertheless made it to production, badged as the Lancia Stratos.

RENAULT RACOON

▼ Just occasionally, highly paid people become too closely involved in the project to which they have been assigned, and say something that subsequently they wish they hadn't. One such person was the spokesman for Renault at the 1993 Geneva Motor Show, when he proudly introduced the bizarre-looking Racoon as 'a firm proposal that could be tomorrow's freedom car'.

Featuring four-wheel drive and a fully watertight body that could be raised using hydraulic jacks to give extra ground-clearance, this go-anywhere, amphibious machine seemed to ask most of the questions that weren't actually on the lips of anyone who was looking at it. The question they must all have been asking after its introduction must have been 'Are you absolutely sure we'll want something like this?' Its non-appearance as a production reality answers this question succinctly.

GHIA MEGASTAR

▲ Rivet-counting car experts would instantly recognise the wheels on the 1977 Ghia Megastar, first shown at the Geneva Auto Show, as coming from the Ford Granada Ghia Mk 1, and whilst most other people would suggest these experts need a more active social-life, their component-spotting would be 100 per cent accurate. The concept also shared many other parts with the mid-seventies executive saloon.

Its appearance, however, was much more revolutionary than its donor vehicle, with a rakish looking body designed by Filippo Sapino. Its front doors were 80 per cent glass, and the interior was made to give the feeling of riding in an executive jet plane. Bizarrely – bearing in mind the fact that concept cars are supposed to wow onlookers as they try to imagine driving a car that has the very latest in dream gizmos, rather than instil a feeling of nervousness – one of the features the designers felt it worthy of drawing attention to was the fire extinguisher fitted in the glove compartment.

VENTURI FETISH

▶ Apart from boasting what many may consider to be a rather brave name, the Venturi Fetish is a remarkable machine that is a genuine first (if one is to believe the manufacturers) in that it is the world's first electric-powered sports car.

Certainly it lacks the awkward bodywork of many electric cars, and looks more than slightly enticing – an impression enhanced yet further by such feats as a 0–60mph sprint time of just 4.3 seconds. No miserable economy electro-shopping trolley ever offered such performance or looks, and allegedly a mere ten minutes plugged into the nearest charger will give a further ten miles' range. Its total range of over 200 miles on a single charge (although presumably with not too many 0–60 dashes) is further encouraging news, but as yet the Fetish is not widely available as a production reality.

The electric future is still, tantalisingly, just around the corner.

DUESENBERG II

▲ There are many myths and legends surrounding the attempted rebirth of America's finest ever marque in 1966. Whether there were 50 examples built, or only the one prototype (which happily still exists, and is on display at the Auburn Cord Duesenberg Museum in Auburn, Indiana), is still hotly debated.

The prototype was based on a Chrysler Imperial, with bodywork heavily restyled by Ghia of Turin to include a 1960s interpretation of such classic Duesenberg styling cues as its radiator grille, and to capture the remnants of the flowing lines of the graceful 1930s front wings. It was not greatly successful as a styling exercise, however, and even its most ardent admirer could not claim that it had much of the grace or beauty of its forebears. Luxury fittings included four-season climate control and electric windows, and it was powered by a 440cu in Chrysler V8, but it never went into production, in spite of alleged interest from potential clients such as Elvis Presley.

FASCINATION

▼ The oft-told story of the Volkswagen Beetle is familiar to most, and many are also aware that in the 1960s and 1970s many time-served Beetles gave up their vital organs to kits, becoming more exciting machines than the Wolfsburg originals. Of all the vehicles powered by VW mechanicals, however, it is doubtful if there are any more bizarre than the Fascination, designed and built in the late 1960s by Paul Lewis of Nebraska.

Built with a fibreglass body, most had four wheels, although the prototype had only three and was originally designed to be powered by a rear-mounted propeller, which fell off on a test-run. Only five were ever built, and happily all still exist, with 60 per cent of this total in the hands of one private collector.

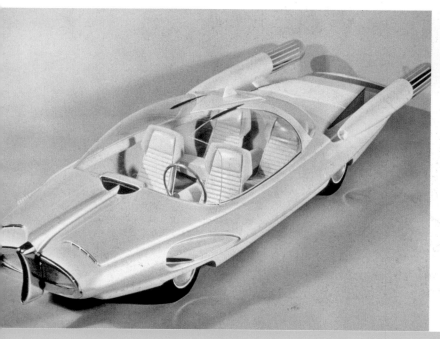

FORD X2000

◀ It's always difficult to predict what we might be driving in 40 years time, although it is probably fair to say that we will all still be driving something: the car has provided too much freedom for us to simply walk away from it due to fossil fuel shortage, global warming, global dimming, or other eco-fears.

Back in 1958, designer Alex Tremulis was working for the Ford Motor Company in Dearborn, Michigan, and he took a stab at what he thought we might all be driving by now. He thought the cars of today – or yesterday, now – would probably look like the Ford X2000. Its vertical oval radiator grille bears more than a passing resemblance to that least favoured aspect of the Ford Edsel, but in other ways it was so futuristic and fantastic it was a dream. Tremulis wasn't to know how dull many of today's cars would turn out: dreams just don't often come true.

Although the X2000 was only ever a clay mock-up, a full size version was finally made many thousands of miles away in Poole, Dorset, by Andy Saunders.

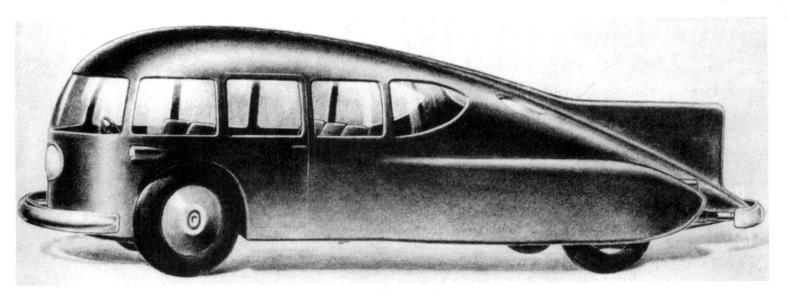

BEL GEDDES CAR NUMBER 8

▲ Perhaps not the most imaginatively named car of all time, the Bel Geddes Car Number 8 was a staggeringly forward-looking machine for 1931. Born in 1893, Norman Bel Geddes was a theatre and industrial designer by trade, who branched out into car, train, gas-range and even revolving restaurant design later in life.

Car Number 8 was a tear-drop shaped machine which came complete with a tail fin, making it look not unlike an automotive bomb, which was capable of carrying eight people in extreme, air-conditioned comfort. Subsequently, he designed a similar-looking double-decker bus, but in neither case was he able to attract the funding required to turn his plans into reality.

PEUGEOT 907

▼ Whilst many concept cars are obviously pure fantasy, others, such as the glorious 907 from Peugeot, look and feel technically possible. Its body is made from very expensive carbon-fibre, which would probably not make it into production, but its 500bhp 6-litre V12 engine, made from two V6 blocks from the 407, is technically feasible. Its rear wheels are driven by a six-speed gearbox mounted on the rear axle, and the interior is more finished than one might expect in a concept car, even down to the specially tailored leather luggage.

Whilst its performance potential is undisputed, and has been demonstrated to a few handpicked motoring writers, no definitive figures have been published.

THE PITS

ASTON MARTIN ZAGATO

▶ Aston Martin are undisputed aristocrats in the field of sports cars, but as with virtually all aristocratic families, there are one or two relatives of which the least said the better.

The sad, malformed recluse that wanders the lofts of Aston Martin's impressive home, Jane Eyre style, is the V8 Zagato, made from 1986–88. Irredeemably ugly, the excuse for such a car ever coming to market was that it came during the mad years of the 1980s boom, when status and the ability to flaunt one's new-found wealth mattered significantly more than good taste. Underneath the hideous coachwork there lurked the pure bloodline of Aston Martin heritage, however. Here was a car that, powered by the Vantage's 5.3-litre V8 engine, could reach 186mph, having dispensed with the first 60 in just 4.8 seconds, whilst the hides of England's finest cattle lined most surfaces of the interior. Just 52 were built.

LADA NIVA

▼ 'Lada. Niva use nor ornament', was the caption to an owner's description of the Russian four-wheel-drive compact in the short-lived *Jalopy* magazine. This may have been a little harsh as a summary of the vehicle's talents, but in the market sector in which it was competing when it appeared in 1978 the opposition was stiff, and the Eastern Bloc three-door Lada always looked the poor relation.

On home territory, where there was no competition, it pleased its owners readily enough (many of whom were just delirious to have any car), but in the West it excelled at nothing, apart from its rate of depreciation after purchase, which meant that after a couple of years they made handy transport for hill-farmers with little cash.

And when its days had finally come to an end, at least the owner could console himself with the comprehensive tool-kit with which all Ladas came, widely regarded as the best kit available on almost any car. Critics would point out, perhaps slightly unkindly, that a tool-kit on a Lada was not a sales gimmick but an absolute essential.

MITSUOKA VIEWT

▲ The Mitsuoka Viewt of 1998 is a rare machine indeed. It is a barely believable blend of Japanese reliable oily bits from a Nissan Micra with an almost-similar body that resembles quite strongly, when squinting, a Jaguar MkII from the 1960s.

Naturally, with so many of the important components coming from a modern supermini, it is hard to recreate fully and with complete conviction the 'grace, pace and space' that the 1960s original had in abundance. One needs look no further from the ground than the wheels to see that something ain't right here, but nevertheless, there are, from certain angles, elements that make one question 'is it or isn't it?'

The answer, of course, has to come back that no, it isn't a Jaguar, but a horrible pastiche that may well look superficially OK on the streets of Tokyo, but would require a brave person to park it outside the gates of the Browns Lane factory in Coventry whence the originals once rolled.

LANCIA BETA

▶ The Lancia Beta was a svelte-looking saloon launched at the 1971 Turin Motor Show. Available with a choice of engines driving the front wheels, a top speed of just under 110mph was available from the 1,800cc version, which, at the time, was highly respectable for a family saloon.

At launch, it all looked so promising. However, everything fell apart in a miserably short time for the owner of a Beta, because, in spite of assurances in the sales literature that 'extensive anti-corrosion protection with electro-phoretic treatment and factory applied under-body sealing' would protect this good-looking Italian thoroughbred, cars were rusting right through in as little as two years.

With their previously enviable reputation now lying in a little reddish brown pile of iron oxide on the floor, the writing was on the wall for Lancia in Britain, where the problem was exacerbated by salt on the roads every winter. Eventually, with sales falling year on year, it proved no longer economically viable to make right-hand drive models for the few customers not put off by the company's new reputation, and Lancia ceased selling cars in the UK.

FORD PINTO

▶ The Pinto of 1971 was a car Ford must have wished many times over it had not built, or about which it had at least listened to the advice it was given.

It was rushed into production in just 25 months rather than the 42 normally taken, because competition in this market sector was very stiff. One of the absolutes set by then Ford boss Lee Iacocca was that it should not cost a dime over $2,000, and so as the price rose close to this limit desirable improvements were ruled out. Unfortunately one such improvement was a safer fuel tank, as it was discovered that in most rear-end crashes this ruptured, invariably causing an inferno. A further problem came if the car was hit in the rear at over 40mph, when the doors would often jam shut, trapping the unfortunate occupants inside.

Whilst it is hard simply to brush aside these shortcomings, many found the car perfectly adequate in every other way, and even Henry Ford II had his very own Pinto, which he often enjoyed driving. There are still devotees out there, who have their own website to promote the car they feel was overshadowed by a problem most motorists hoped never to experience.

HINDUSTAN AMBASSADOR

▶ Is it a 1957 Morris Oxford Series III or a Hindustan Ambassador? Lift the bonnet, and if there's an Isuzu 1,800cc petrol or diesel engine in the near antique engine bay it's a genuine Calcutta original. While most cars fade away into distant memories once production ceases, a select few have all their tooling shipped abroad and carry on for many more decades, being churned out in countries where the motorists are less demanding than in the West. The Morris Oxford thus became the Hindustan Ambassador.

There was an attempt to import examples to Britain in the early 1990s, but once people realised it still had cart-spring suspension, drum brakes all round, and very little more sophistication than it had four decades earlier, but was costing as much as a modern Western car, its olde worlde appeal rapidly fell away and few examples found buyers.

ALFASUD

◄ The Alfasud promised great things when it was launched in 1972, but it failed to deliver on many. Built in a new factory just south of Naples, using new techniques and automated machines, including those used on body assembly, the recipe sounded a good one, and when the press tested it they were glowing in their praise. Its Boxer engine was a beauty, and its handling was fantastic.

Ownership, however, was a different matter. The cute body, designed by Giugiaro of Ital Design, looked like a highly usable hatchback, competing with the new Volkswagen Golf; but it wasn't, and its boot was both awkward and small. Reliability problems were an issue also, but the huge defect which killed many Alfasuds ahead of their time was rust, which attacked almost every area of the car with the sort of infectious spread normally reserved for an outbreak of acne on a teenager, reducing the promising little family car to MoT failure in a depressingly short period.

TALBOT RANCHO

▼ There can have been few cars throughout the history of motorised transport more cynically conceived, and ultimately disappointing, than 1977's Talbot Rancho.

Looking like a vehicle ready for a trip around the globe, the Rancho was in fact merely a tarted-up Simca van, made to look macho by the addition of large amounts of black rubber fittings, roof-bars, rugged-looking look-alike alloy wheels, and a few other cheap add-ons. It may have looked like it was four-wheel drive, but guess what? It wasn't: just the front wheels received what miserable power was on offer from its puny 1,442cc four-cylinder engine.

Sold as a lifestyle vehicle, it was in fact a complete sham and a travesty.

VAUXHALL VICTOR F TYPE

▲ At the end of the Second World War the British motor industry started up again, initially building pre-war designs. However, the pressure was on manufacturers to export or die, so when new designs were penned they were aimed at overseas sales, and in particular the USA. Increasingly, British cars tried – not always successfully, as in the case of the Austin Atlantic – to imitate American designs and appeal to US tastes.

One imitator was the F Type Victor, which was launched by Vauxhall with much glitz and glamour in 1957 and came complete with gaudy chrome, awkward styling, and a wrap-around windscreen. Whilst beauty may be in the eye of the beholder, rust-proofing should have been the responsibility of the manufacturer, but due to their sourcing inferior steel cheaply from Belgium, and the fact that most cars were going abroad where roads were not salted every winter, this seems to have been overlooked, and the cars rapidly gained an unenviable reputation as miserable rust-boxes – a reputation it has taken Vauxhall decades to live down.

IRAN KHODRO PEYKAN 1600

▼ In 1965 the Rootes Group launched the Hillman Hunter, an unremarkable four-door family saloon with a variety of engines which ploughed up and down the roads of Britain until 1979, when it was finally killed off (and not before time, as it was by then heavily out-classed by almost everything on sale).

It was also exported to all the territories that Rootes Group products were sold in, and furthermore enjoyed a considerably longer lifespan under the assumed name of Peykan, sold in Iran initially as CKD (completely knocked down) kits which were assembled locally. After a short break during the Iranian revolution at the end of the 1970s, it was manufactured there as a home-grown product, only finally ceasing production in 2005.

Whilst it is still possible to see many Peykans plying for trade on the streets of Tehran as taxis, this does not mean they were good cars, but simply that they are owned by people who are too poor to replace them and are therefore obliged to keep the old jalopy going come what may.

SUZUKI X-90

◄ The X-90 from Suzuki appeared to be the result of a late-night meeting between a domineering marketing department, a young and eager-to-please designer, and unwilling engineers. Notionally a 4x4, it was aimed at thrusting and aspiring youngsters who wanted (apparently) a sports car during the week, in which to cruise around their chosen city, and a 4x4 for the weekend, in which to go off-road or tow the jet-skis down to the coast to annoy everyone else on the beach.

Based on the not-much-better Vitara, it was a risible car, which the style-conscious (at whom it was aimed) almost universally loathed. Its off-road ability was severely limited, but its aspirations in that direction ensured it was not much better on the tarmac, and opinion generally labelled it a hairdresser's car – ie suitable only for poseurs rather than for the tasks originally envisaged by the marketing people. It was also an undisputed sales flop, with just 1,500 examples selling in the UK between 1996 and 1998.

VELOREX

▼ Built in Hradec Kralove, Czechoslovakia, the Velorex, available from 1953 to 1971, was without doubt one of the most crude vehicles of its generation, if not of all time. Available with a choice of three different-sized JAWA motorcycle engines, the 125cc and 250cc single cylinder versions had a kick-starter modified for hand use, whilst the 250cc twin cylinder version – calling it the deluxe version is too proud a boast – had an electric starter. The whole machine was built around a cage of welded steel tubes covered with a vinyl-like material called 'Igelit'. It is perhaps viewed as one step up, albeit a very small one, from a motorcycle, and one cannot help but feel that the Czechs who bought it in the numbers they did may not have done so had they been able to buy cars built outside the Eastern Bloc.

AMC PACER

▲ The 1970s were not an easy time for many motor manufacturers, and most companies turned out at least one dullard that they now choose to try and forget. Few, however, can equal the appalling Pacer from the American Motors Corporation for sheer unworthiness of a place on the road.

To paraphrase an ancient saying, desperation is the mother of mistakes, and at the time AMC were desperate. The oil crisis was making their large and thirsty cars less attractive than the European and Japanese imports that were gaining a foothold in the homeland, so they had a go at building something in a similar mould. Their offering, the Pacer, was a blobby hatchback which may have looked smaller in the pictures but was still large by anything other than American standards, and with an entry level engine capacity of 3.8 litres, economy figures had to be seen as relative. An atrocious car in every respect, it was no match for the imports with which it was supposed to do battle, and after five years of low sales AMC admitted defeat and allowed it to die.

PREMIER PADMINI

▼ Motorists in India have a bewildering choice of vehicles from which to choose, from modern product such as Toyotas, Fords, and Hyundais, to antique basics such as the Premier Padmini, derived from the 1962 Fiat 1100. Its 1,089cc engine that puts out a miserable 40bhp is considerably older still, having first seen service in 1953.

Crude simplicity is the hallmark of the Padmini, from its cart-spring suspension at the rear through to virtually every mechanical aspect, in which its manufacturers, rather than being somewhat ashamed, find virtue by pointing out that it is a vehicle which can be readily serviced by the most basically equipped mechanic. Fit and finish are further victims in comparison to more modern vehicles, as is its leisurely performance with a top speed of 65mph.

Perhaps the best way to describe a customer who might be drawn to such a contraption is as someone who needs a boot, but has little loot to put in it. It is a machine whose time has long since passed, and does not fare well in comparison to other cars on sale today.

AUSTIN ATLANTIC

◄ Named after the stretch of water which separated the car from the principal market Austin were aiming at with its A90, the Atlantic was part of the immediate post-war export-or-die era. Its styling was an unhappy blend of American extrovert with British reserve, and as such failed to find many takers on either side of the Atlantic Ocean in the four years after its launch in 1948 before it was quietly dropped.

Its suspension was deliberately soft, as it was felt that this would be more to the American taste – but its lacklustre 88bhp, 2.6-litre, four-cylinder engine, giving leisurely acceleration and a top speed of just 84mph, was most definitely not. Rust-proofing, while not a great problem for cars destined for the US, where salt is not liberally shovelled over every inch of tarmac when the temperature drops near freezing, was distinctly lacking on the Austin A90, resulting in the examples that stayed in Britain dissolving rapidly into little piles of rust, and there are very few original examples now left anywhere in the UK.

NISSAN TERRANO

▼ 'Avoid at all costs' is not what any manufacturer wants to see written about its cars, but 'the Good, the Bad & the Ugly' section of the highly respected *Car* magazine gave exactly this advice regarding the Nissan Terrano, which, it says, is good in the mud but awful everywhere else, summing it up by calling it 'Britain's worst car'.

Available with either a 2.7-litre diesel or 3-litre petrol engine, it is capable of 105mph in 154bhp petrol form, and under normal conditions its rear wheels do the driving: the driver can summon help from the fronts as well with a separate lever.

Whilst in absolute terms, *Car*'s criticisms are perhaps a little unfair, in the company of its rivals it is less competent than most, which is more a reflection on how good the competition is than how bad the Terrano is.

MASERATI BITURBO

▼ For most people the name Maserati conjures up exotic images of fast, highly desirable and deeply exotic Italian sports cars, but for much of the 1980s it conjured up rather different images, of lacklustre machines that had lost their design direction and a company that appeared to have fired all of its quality control inspectors.

The car guilty of so besmirching the illustrious reputation of the once proud company was the Biturbo, which came in a variety of shapes and sizes: a saloon or coupé, with V6 or V8 engines, and a range of body-kits designed to differentiate the models and hide the dull anonymity of the basic car. Different, alluring names were given to special editions, such as the Kamal, Shamal, and Ghibli, but the basic machine remained much the same, with tweaks and body modifications, and in this way Maserati somehow managed to limp through the 1980s and much of the 1990s until the glorious 3200GT was launched by a vastly different company now owned by Fiat, and the work of restoring the company's reputation began in earnest.

BMW 600

◄ In modern times we have come to associate the name of BMW with prestige and sporty cars, luxury, refinement, and desirability. All of these qualities can be found in spadefuls in modern BMWs, but every car manufacturer has skeletons in the cupboard, models of which they are less proud and which vary dramatically with today's image as portrayed by the guys in Marketing. For BMW, one such car is the 600.

Designed by Willy Black, it was an enlarged Isetta, with four wheels, four seats, an extra door, and extra ccs courtesy of the 582cc engine from the R76 motorcycle to propel the extra weight to its none too electrifying top speed of 64mph. The problem was, however, that while the Isetta had a cute appeal to it, the 600 looked overweight and ungainly in spite of Michelotti helping with the design, and it did not fare well against cars such as the VW Beetle. Launched in 1957, it sold just 34,000 in the two years it was available.

FIAT STRADA

► 'A car to take Fiat into the eighties' was how Fiat proudly announced their new family hatchback in 1979. It looked modern, had the very best television commercial ever made to launch it, which even today still wins praise, and was actually built by robots.

The subtext of this last boast was 'no more Friday-afternoon cars'. Everything would be right, first time, every time. With prices starting at £3,034 for a three-door hatchback, one would have thought Fiat executives would have been rubbing their hands with glee, waiting to clean up in the sales charts, but it was not to be. Whilst it may have been designed by a computer, we all know that with computers, rubbish in equals rubbish out, and the car's designers must have fed the poor computer a diet of pure garbage. So bad was it that Fiat were actually issuing dealerships with service bulletins advising about recurring problems and how to rectify them before the first cars had even been delivered. Rust was another major enemy, and the Strada failed comprehensively, because of this and a plethora of other faults, to live up to the hype that had accompanied its launch.

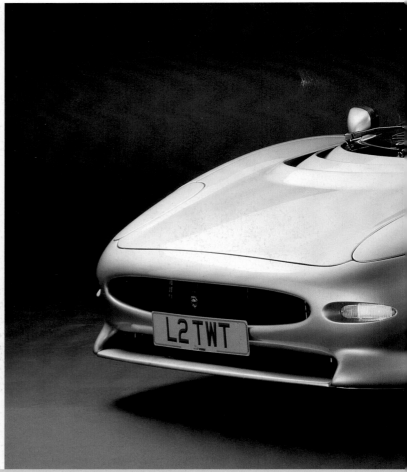

TRABANT

▶ Most people have at some stage in their lives criticised one car or another and called it rubbish, but in the case of the Trabant – or as the Eastern Bloc trendies called them, Trabbies – this title was particularly appropriate, not merely because almost every aspect of the car could be improved, but mainly because its bodywork was made from compressed cardboard, cemented together with glue.

The car also had a very nasty smoking habit, courtesy of its appallingly crude two-stroke, two-cylinder engine, which was only replaced by a proper VW engine in the last couple of years of the car's life. Built in Zwickau from 1958–91, its fate was sealed the moment the Berlin Wall came down and the residents of East Germany had access to proper cars.

JAGUAR XJ220

▼ The Jaguar XJ220 story is one of woe, where a great idea became a huge nightmare in almost every sense of the word.

Originally launched in 1988 to great applause, here was a 48-valve V12 powered four-wheel-drive supercar with a proud name and heritage, which would go on to become the world's fastest car, with a top speed of 220mph – hence the name. But it never quite turned out like that.

Investors fought to lay down their £50,000 deposits on a car that would cost them each £403,000 on delivery. But the problems of converting dream-car into production reality led to a depletion by 50 per cent in the number of promised engine cylinders, and a similar reduction in the percentage of driven wheels. It didn't even reach the promised top speed: in the end 213mph was its limit, which was respectable enough until a few months later when the smaller, leaner, and more handsome McLaren trashed the overgrown and under-loved Jaguar. To pile insult upon injury, by the time the Jaguar was ready many of the investors, who were really no more than speculators, had lost their shirts in the market crash at the end of the 1980s and could no longer afford to buy the car.

MITSUOKA GALUE II

▲ According to the company's website, Galue means 'doing it in my own way' in Japanese, or, as they interpret it, 'This is my own life, my own philosophy'. This, presumably, is the excuse for a 2-litre, six-cylinder engine driving something that looks like a cross between a 1950s Wolseley police car and a Bentley S1, with a few other influences and styling cues thrown in for good measure. Underneath all this faux pastiche is a somewhat less classic Nissan Crew.

Mitsuoka is a small Japanese manufacturer building up to 100 cars per month, aiming to offer the ambience of a classic British saloon with the comfort and reliability of modern Japanese running gear and electronics. Whilst from certain angles it could be confused, at a distance of more than 20 yards, for a genuine classic, too much of the modern Nissan remains to convince any but the least observant.

AUSTIN PRINCESS

▼ The Austin Princess was a shockingly bad car in every conceivable way, and found most of its owners only through a misplaced sense of patriotism. Built between 1975 and 1982, its Harris Mann designed sloping rear led one to believe it might at least have the useful function of a hatchback, but … no, only an awkward-sized boot.

The ergonomics inside were appalling, the build quality was even worse, whilst the ride was just atrocious, and gave the impression that the entire engineering department must have been on another of BL's legendary strikes throughout its entire development period. Rivals at Ford must have suffered near fatal injuries trying to suppress their mirth when it was launched, especially when they saw its TV advert, which described it, tellingly, as 'Not the car for Mr Average'. Enough said.

TALBOT TAGORA

▲ At the beginning of the 1980s, all the major manufacturers were still fielding offerings in the large executive class. Rover had their sleek, if poorly built 800 and Sterling series, Ford had their Granada range, Volvo the 760, and Vauxhall the Carlton and Senator. Talbot, the ex-Rootes Group of companies recently bought by Peugeot, saw that they needed to be in this market in order to add something to their dowdy image, and the car they brought out was the truly awful Tagora.

The general expectations of the British car-buying public were not especially high in 1982, but even this was insufficient to tease the poor sales figures up from a mere 6,000 per year for the four years it was in production. Powered by either a 2.2-litre four-cylinder engine or a 2.7-litre V6, it had the trimmings of luxury, with electric windows and power steering, but its styling department appeared to have completed their artwork during one of the many blackouts that were part of the late 1970s socio-industrial landscape.

The few private individuals who, for whatever reason, ended up owning a Tagora had as their one consolation the incredibly poor rustproofing and general lousy build-quality which removed most examples from the road in a remarkably short time.

FORD CAPRI 1300

▼ If the Capri was the poor man's Ferrari, then the 1,300cc version was very much the poor man's Capri. The Capri had a lovely long bonnet suggesting power, sport, and other predominantly male, machismo themes, which, when it was covering a 3-litre V6 Essex engine, it was largely able to live up to.

But with the asthmatic 1,300 crossflow Escort engine under the muscular bonnet, this sorry little powerplant looked very shrunken, shrivelled, and puny, a perception further confirmed when it was coaxed into life and asked to summon its 57bhp to propel the family 'sports car'. With pressed-steel wheels, and lacking any luxury fittings of any description, this was a car that had been built down to a price, and that price was just too low. Whilst wanting to be inclusive and offer Capri ownership to as many of the populace as possible was a laudable aim, debasing the Mustang-inspired Capri – which, when fitted with more than 2 litres, was undeniably a good car for its time – proved to be a bad move, and resulted in a very poor vehicle.

POSTSCRIPT

After all the glamour, the fins, the spoilers, the super-wide tyres, traction-control systems, and all the other gizmos and gadgets found on today's supercars, it may come as a surprise to read that the beaming Stelios Haji-Iannou, pictured here, is smiling because the humble Mercedes A-Class at his side is actually the fastest car of them all.

As everyone knows, the fastest car on the road is always a hire car.

BIBLIOGRAPHY

Automania Julian Pettifer & Nigel Turner, Collins 1984.
The Beaulieu Encyclopaedia of the Automobile Edited by G. N. Georgano, The Stationery Office 2000.
Cars that Time Forgot Giles Chapman, Paragon 1997.
A Century of Sports Cars Derek Avery, Brockhampton Press 1998.
Classic British Cars Graham Robson & Michael Ware, Abbeydale Press 2000.
Classic & Sportscar A–Z of Cars 1945–70 Michael Sedgwick & Mark Gilies, Bay View Books 1993.
The Complete Encyclopaedia of Motorcars 1885 to the Present Edited by G. N. Georgano, Ebury Press 1970.
Concept Cars Chris Rees, Barnes & Noble 2000.
Dream Cars Andrew Frankel, Weidenfeld & Nicolson 1997.
Encyclopaedia of the Car Grange Books 1993.
The Encyclopaedia of Classic Cars Edited by Kevin Brazendale, Blitz Editions 1999.
The Encyclopaedia of Classic Cars Martin Buckley, Lorenz Books 1997.
Encyclopedia of the World's Classic Cars Graham Robson, Galley Press 1982.
The Ford In Britain File Eric Dymock, Dove Publishing 2002.
High and Mighty Keith Bradsher, Perseus Books 2002.
The Illustrated Encyclopaedia of Automobiles David Burgess Wise, Hamlyn 1979.
The Renault File Eric Dymock, Dove Publishing 1998.
Sports Car Classics Iain Ayre, Lorenz Books 2003.
Sports Cars on Road & Track Ray Hutton, Hamlyn 1973.
Star Cars Beki Adam, Osprey 1987.
Stars, Cars & Infamy Martin Buckley, Motorbooks International 2003.
The World of Cars Roy Bacon, Sunbust Books 1995.
Auoindex.org
3wheelers.com

ACKNOWLEDGEMENTS

With thanks to:

Nick Mason
Andy Willsheer
Jonathan Day
BigFoot 4x4 Inc.
Chris Rees
Erik van Ingen
    Schenau
Mick Walsh
Jon Pressnell
Nick Georgano
Rick Woodbury

Mark Gerisch
Giles Chapman
Harold Pace
Jac Gerken
Elvis Payne
3Wheelers.com
Peter Vincent
Ron Kimball
Simon Clay
Tim Cottingham
Christopher Mohs
Dan Crosby
Bob Stuart

John Lakey
Hisahi Ishihara
Dave Mann
Russ Meeks
Claudia Haase
Terry Pudwell
Mike Richards
Jim Dudley
Artiagini Anna
Jonah Ansell
Jean-Pierre Kraemer
Ana Rollan
Jon Bill

Henry M Caroselli
Eileen Carpenter
Robin Wallis
Naseem Ullah
Motoring Picture Library,
    National Motor
    Museum, Beaulieu
Auburn Cord
    Duesenberg Museum
Harry Ransom Humanities
    Research Center,
    The University of
    Texas at Austin

INDEX